24
TABLE SAW
PROJECTS

PERCY W. BLANDFORD

TAB BOOKS Inc.

Blue Ridge Summit, PA

FIRST EDITION
SECOND PRINTING

Copyright © 1988 by TAB BOOKS Inc.
Printed in the United States of America

Library of Congress Cataloging in Publication Data

Blandford, Percy W.
24 table saw project / by Percy W. Blandford.
        p. cm.
    Includes index.
    ISBN 0-8306-2964-5 (pbk.)
    1. Woodworking. I. Title. II. Title: Twenty-four table saw
        projects.
    TT180.B617   1987   87-29047
    684.1′042—dc19   CIP

Questions regarding the content of this book
should be addressed to:

Reader Inquiry Branch
Editorial Department
TAB BOOKS Inc.
Blue Ridge Summit, PA 17294-0214

Cover photographs courtesy of Delta International Machinery Corp.

Contents

Introduction

A TABLE SAW IS ONE OF THE CENTRAL AND MOST-used power tools in a woodworking shop. Besides its obvious use for cutting wood to width and thickness, it can have many other uses that are not always appreciated. Blades of different types will cut various materials, and some can be used for grooving and rabbeting. The rise-and-fall facility allows cuts to be made to controlled depths, while the standard fences and guides can be supplemented by store-bought and shopmade equipment or improvisations. A surprising number of joints can be cut completely (or almost so) on the table saw.

Some owners tend to use their table saw for simple cuts only, but there are other functions it can perform as well as, or better than, some other equipment. The saw is particularly valuable for repetition work where, for instance, a large number of identical tenons have to be cut. The use of guides ensures accuracy every time.

Where a project requires a large number of matching, but nonstandard, strips, only a table saw can produce these accurately and quickly. With a table saw, you can re-use wood by converting parts of discarded furniture and other structures into important parts of new projects.

This is not a book on table saw techniques, although some guidance is offered in a few cases. It is mainly an ideas book. Anyone wishing to learn about table saw techniques should read the companion *The Table Saw Book,* TAB book No. 2789, by R.J. De Cristoforo.

While very few projects can be made with only a table saw, for the items described here, the table saw plays a major part, and all of them require its use. As will be seen in several projects, variations and modifications are described. I hope you will not only make some of the items described, but use them as a base to develop your own ideas. That way you will get the satisfaction of producing something that is uniquely your own.

Descriptions of each project include a picture and sufficient drawings and step-by-step instructions for the article to be made. There is a materials list, where appropriate. All sizes are in inches. Thicknesses and widths are exact, but lengths are full in order to allow for cutting.

There is something here for all degrees of skill and types of equipment. The beginner should not be deterred from tackling what might seem too ambitious a project. If you follow the instructions a step at a time, you will achieve results that will surprise. For more instruction on general woodworking, see the other books of interest listing at the back of this book.

Glass-Fronted Display Board

CUTTING RABBETS FOR A PICTURE FRAME IS AN obvious use for a table saw. A fine-toothed saw and a fairly slow feed should result in a satisfactory finish on most woods, without further treatment. This project (Fig. 1-1) takes the work a stage further, because the glass front stands in front of a *display board* on which can be mounted anything you wish to show and protect, such as butterflies, dried flowers, knots, and other memorabilia. The gap between the glass and the display board can be set to suit the amount of projection of the intended display. The overall size may be whatever is necessary, but for the following instructions it is assumed that overall the frame will be 18 inches by 24 inches, and the gap between the glass and the board will be ½ inch.

Any wood may be used, but the best results come from using a hardwood with a close grain. The back may be plywood or hardboard.

1. Prepare sufficient overlength stock, sawed and planed to width and thickness.

2. Cut the first rabbet in each piece in two stages (Fig. 1-2A and B). Allow for the thickness of the glass and a ½-inch fillet.

3. Cut the second rabbet into the first (Fig. 1-2C and D), allowing for the thickness of the backboard and enough overlap for screwing through.

4. Cut strips for fillets (using waste from the frames) to allow for the glass thickness, and to come level with the inside edge of the frame (Fig. 1-2E).

5. Chamfer the front edge by tilting the saw or its fence, then plane and sand all the parts that will be exposed (Fig. 1-2F).

6. Cut the backboard to size, so it can be used for checking the size and squareness of the frame parts.

7. Using the backboard as a guide to size (Fig. 1-2G), mark the miters and cut them.

8. It may be satisfactory to bring the miters of a light frame together and nail or screw in both directions, but for most frames more reinforcement would be advisable.

Fig. 1-1. A glass-fronted display board protects exhibits.

9. One or two dowels may be driven through holes square to the meeting surfaces (Fig. 1-2H), or one can be driven each way (Fig. 1-2J).

10. Another way of strengthening the corners is to put pieces of 1/16-inch veneer in saw cuts (Fig. 1-2K).

11. Fit the fillets with a few pins, so they can be withdrawn easily if you ever have to replace the glass. Slide a light hammer along a piece of card (Fig. 1-2L) to minimize the risk of cracking the glass.

12. When you have prepared your exhibit and the front of the backboard, use fine screws to fix it to the frame at about 6-inch intervals.

Materials List for Glass-Fronted Display Board

2 pieces	1⅜	×	1⅜	× 20
2 pieces	1⅜	×	1⅜	× 26
2 pieces	⅜	×	½	× 18
2 pieces	⅜	×	½	× 24
1 piece	17	×	23	× ¼ plywood

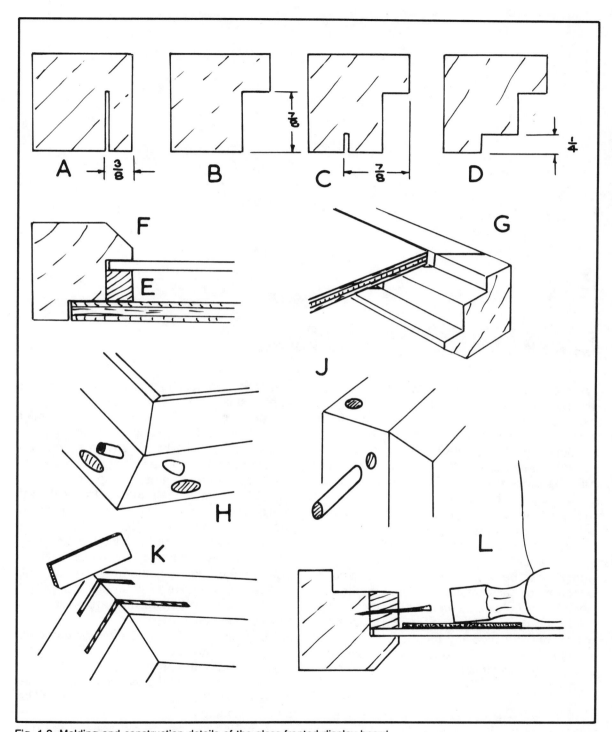

Fig. 1-2. Molding and construction details of the glass-fronted display board.

2
Laundry Box

A TABLE SAW WILL CUT GROOVES FOR PANELS, and this *laundry box* (Fig. 2-1) uses four corner posts with grooves as the main parts of the assembly. With the sizes suggested (Fig. 2-2), the box is suitable for use in a bedroom or bathroom for items to be washed, but it could be made to other sizes for different purposes, including a small box to stand on a table to contain small articles or a much larger version for use in the garden or shop. Section sizes may be altered, but construction will be the same.

The laundry box may be made of softwood, with plywood panels, although a light hardwood will be more satisfactory. In any case, the finished box should be painted, so wood of mixed colors or textures will not matter. Exact sizes are not critical, but grooving must suit the panels chosen. If the box will be used in wet conditions, use a water-resistant glue and exterior grade plywood.

1. Prepare the wood for the corner posts, with grooves to suit the panels (Fig. 2-3A), made with several adjoining straight cuts or with a *wobble saw*.

2. Cut the panels to size. They determine the box's size, but need not reach the bottoms of the grooves. The box is shown square, but the length and width may differ if you wish or if the box is to fit into a certain space.

3. Assemble the panels in the posts with glue and add square strips at top and bottom between the posts (Figs. 2-2A and 2-3B). Make up opposite sides, then cut and fit the bottom (Fig. 2-3C), which would be difficult to fit in if all four sides were brought together first. This will hold the assembly square while the glue sets.

4. Top and bottom rims are similar. Cut strips to miter on top of the posts (Fig. 2-2C and 2-3D). Round or *chamfer* top and bottom outer edges of the box top strips, but only round the upper edges of the bottom strips. Fit the strips in place with glue and pins, which may be set below the surface and covered with wood filler before painting.

5. Use the saw to cut square feet (Fig.

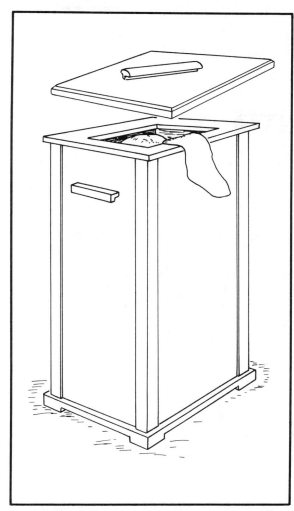

Fig. 2-1. A laundry box with lid, made with plywood panels.

2-2D). Fit them in place with glue and pins. Take sharpness off edges that will come into contact with a carpet.

6. The box can be used with an open top, but a lid is shown, with a plywood panel framed all around. Prepare sufficient strips to the section shown (Fig. 2-2E). Make the groove to about half the thickness of the plywood to be used. Cut rabbets to fit into the box top.

7. Miter the corners to a size that will allow the lid to fit easily into the box. There is no need for a very close fit, and it should be possible to turn and fit the lid at any position.

8. Make the plywood panel to fit into the lid frame. It is important that the top finishes level and close to the frame. It does not matter if the wood does not reach the bottoms of the grooves (Fig. 2-2F).

9. Chamfer or round the outer edges of the lid. Glue alone should be sufficient to hold the lid parts together, but if necessary pins may be driven across the miters.

10 The box can be lifted by its rim, but handles may be made and screwed to opposite sides (Fig. 2-2G). Make the type shown by rabbeting a strip. Chamfer the edges and bevel the ends (Fig. 2-3E).

11. A matching handle for the lid may be fitted diagonally. It has two rabbets and surface chamfering to match the side handles (Fig. 2-3F).

12. Remove all sharp angles and edges before sanding and painting.

Materials List for Laundry Box

4 posts	1¼ × 1¼ × 27	
4 panels	27 × 14 × ¼ plywood	
8 rims	½ × 1⅞ × 17	
8 fillets	½ × ½ × 15	
4 feet	½ × 1⅞ × 1⅞	
4 lid frames	⅞ × 1¼ × 15	
1 lid panel	14 × 14 × ⅜ plywood	
1 bottom	14 × 14 × ⅜ plywood	

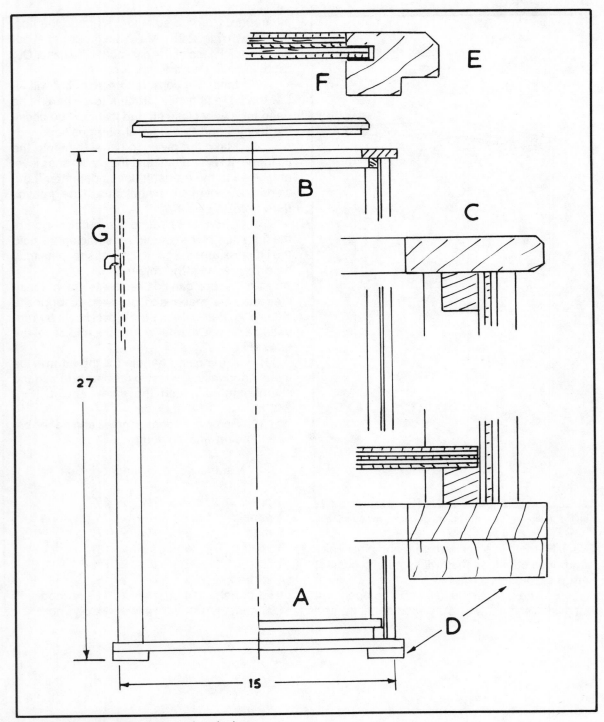

Fig. 2-2. Sizes and sections for the laundry box.

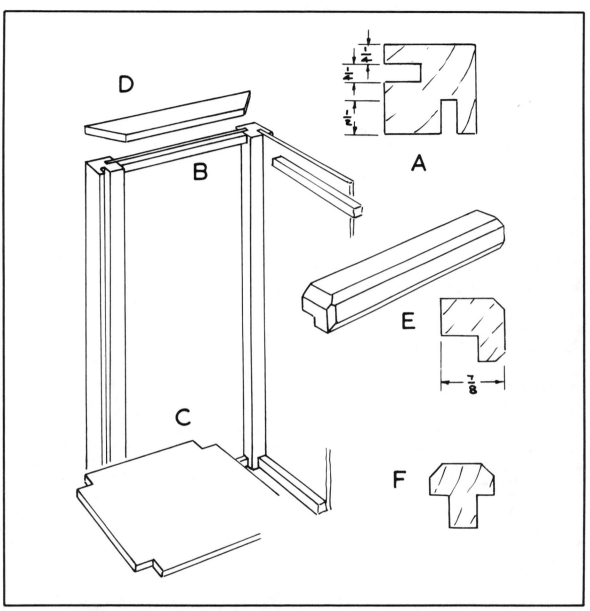

Fig. 2-3. Laundry box assembly and sections of parts.

3

Double-Door Cabinet

ACUPBOARD OR CABINET THAT CAN BE CLOSED with doors is useful for many purposes in the kitchen, shop, garage, or almost anywhere in the home. With shelves inside, many items can be stored and protected by the doors from dust and dirt. Even if cleanliness is not the first consideration, doors will hide what might otherwise be an untidy collection of assorted things.

This cabinet (Fig. 3-1) is of straightforward construction, with paneled doors. Most of the work may be done with a table saw, a planer, and a few hand tools. A cabinet of average size is shown (Fig. 3-2), but the same construction could be used for very different sizes. A narrower cabinet might have a single door.

The choice of wood will depend on the intended use. Softwood may be painted, but polished hardwood is attractive in any room. Suggested wood sections may be cut on the saw, but if you want to make the cabinet a different size or use up wood of slightly different sizes, that is possible.

1. Mark out a pair of sides first, because they determine most other sizes (Fig. 3-3A). Rabbet the rear edges to suit a plywood back. The *dado joints* could be cut across with the saw and the waste between removed with a chisel. The design shows the bottom cut square across, so the cabinet can stand, but if it is to hang on a wall, bottom edges might be beveled the same as the top.

2. Make the three lower shelves to fit into the dadoes to come level with the front edges of the sides.

3. Make the top shelf wide enough to overhang the door by about ¼ inch and extend over the sides a short distance (Fig. 3-3B).

4. Prepare the back, ready to fit into its rabbets when the other parts are assembled, so it will hold them square.

5. When you assemble, drive two thin screws upwards (Fig. 3-3C) into each shelf joint at bottom and top. Glue alone should be sufficient at the intermediate joints.

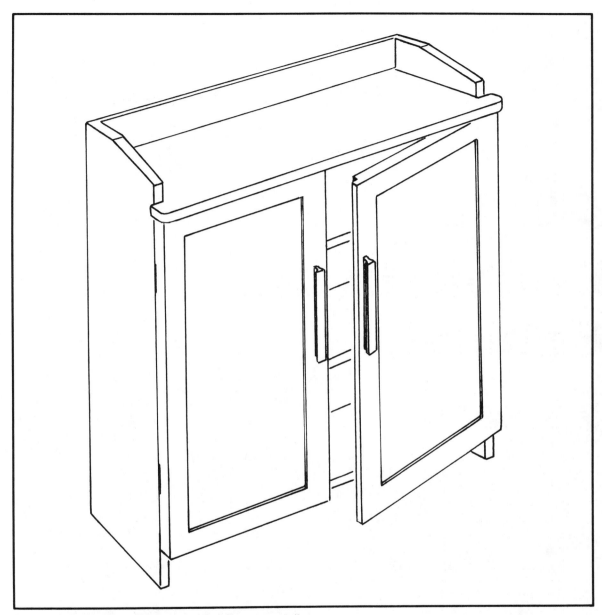

Fig. 3-1. A double-door cabinet to stand or hang on a wall.

6. Prepare wood for the door frames. The grooves will be used to take tenons as well as the ¼-inch plywood panels—a depth of ½ inch should be satisfactory (Fig. 3-3D). The doors may merely meet at the center, but it will be better if they overlap. So the front appearance is the same, the *stile* of one door should be made wider to allow for the rabbet (Fig 3-3E). Make the doors to overlap the bottom shelf by ¼ inch. Leave the stiles long until after assembly, then plane them level after the glue has set.

7. As you assemble the doors, the ply-

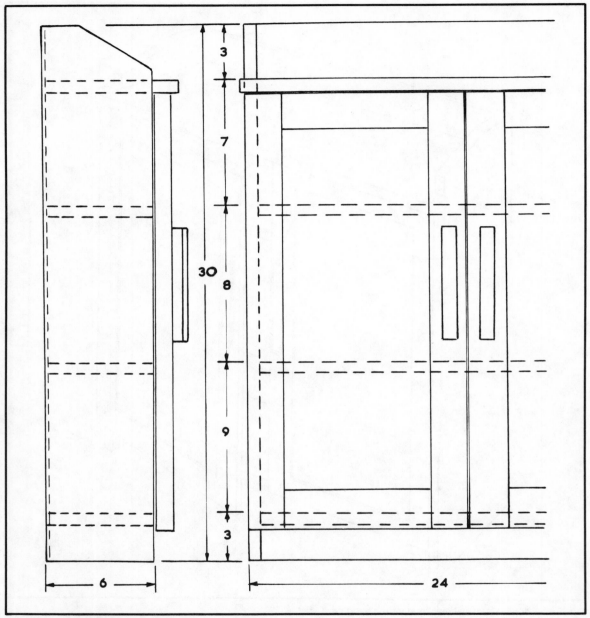

Fig. 3-2. Sizes of the double-door cabinet.

wood panels need not reach the bottoms of the grooves, but the tenon joints (Fig. 3-3F) should pull tight. Thoroughly glue the frame joints, but the panels can have spots of glue in the grooves at fairly wide intervals, to avoid the problem of

excess glue squeezing out and having to be removed.

8. Two 3-inch hinges each side may be flush on the doors, but let into the sides (Fig. 3-3G). At the center, use a small bolt, spring

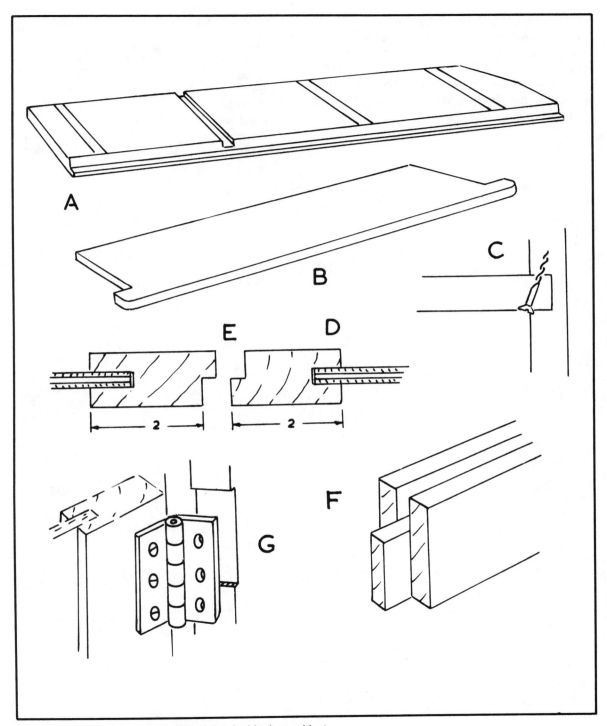

Fig. 3-3. Parts, sections, and details of the double-door cabinet.

11

catch, or magnetic fastener to hold the door with the outward facing rabbet to one shelf; use a similar fastener on the other door or a latch controlled by a knob to fasten one door to the other. There may be turned wood knobs on the doors, or you could make handles with double rabbets on the saw.

Materials List for Double-Door Cabinet

2 sides			×	6	×	31
3 shelves			×	5¾	×	24
1 shelf			×	7½	×	26
1 back	24	×	30	×	¼ plywood
3 door stiles	1	×	2	×	27
1 door stile	1	×	2⅜	×	27
4 door rails	1	×	2	×	11
2 door panels	10	×	23	×	¼ plywood

Checker-Top Magazine Table

A SMALL TABLE IS OFTEN DESCRIBED AS A *COFFEE table,* and if it has a shelf underneath, it makes a good chairside table for storing magazines as well as a place for cups of coffee.

One operation that a saw table does well is to make any number of pieces of wood of a uniform size, either in strips or cut across to produce squares. This table (Fig. 4-1) is intended for magazine storage and has a top decorated with a pattern of squares within a border. These and several other parts are cut at one setting of 2-inch width. Of course, you could make a square table with a chessboard top in the same way, but the checker arrangement on this table is intended as decoration, with the squares cut from the same wood and mounted with the grain in alternate directions.

The size must allow for a regular 2-inch spacing within the border, as in the drawing (Fig. 4-2A), so the sizes may be varied in 2-inch steps, if you prefer a different size. Beneath the table is a shelf made up of a number of slats, also 2 inches wide, supported between 2-inch rails and

providing space for a large number of magazines, newspapers, and other things (Fig. 4-2B).

The checker pattern looks best if you use a hardwood with a prominent grain. The ½-inch border strip could be a darker wood, or the same wood stained before fitting. Other parts will probably be the same wood, but may be different for a special effect. The top has a ½-inch plywood base, and this (with its surface pattern) should be made first, and the sizes of other parts matched to it.

1. Cut pieces for the ½-inch inner border from ¼-inch stock, then set the saw fence to 2 inches and keep it at that until you have cut all the top parts and sufficient strips of the same thickness for the shelf slats and the pieces for the rails.

2. From the strips, cut enough squares to fill the top. If you use a sharp fine-toothed blade, there should be little need to plane or sand edges and they will all remain a uniform size.

3. Have the ½-inch plywood slightly too

13

Fig. 4-1. This magazine table has a checker design top and a shelf made from slats.

big, but start gluing on the borders and squares at a squared corner. Check the length the squares will occupy and miter the border pieces to suit. Bed everything adequately in glue, press the parts together, and cover the whole top in one operation. Clamp the assembly with a board to spread the pressure. Weights on top may provide sufficient clamping.

4. Trim the edges square. Sand the top surface level. An *orbital sander* should provide a good finish without much risk of sanding lines showing across the grain of squares.

5. There are two ways of arranging an edge. There may be a ¼-inch strip glued and pinned on, with mitered corners and top and bottom surfaces level (Fig. 4-3A). Or, it may be bet-

ter to make a similar border that stands up about ⅜-inch with a rounded top (Fig. 4-3B).

6. The legs are 1½-inch-square, without added decoration. Mark them out (Fig. 4-3C). Leave a little extra at the tops for trimming level after assembly.

7. Mark top and bottom rails to match. Allow for the legs being set in 1½ inches from the edges at the top. Cut ¼-inch grooves in the lower long rails (Fig. 4-3D) to take the slats.

8. Rail-to-leg joints could be mortise and tenons, but dowels are suggested (Fig. 4-3E).

9. Prepare the top rails for *pocket screws* into the top (Fig. 4-3F). A screw near the end of each rail and another at the center of the long rail should be sufficient.

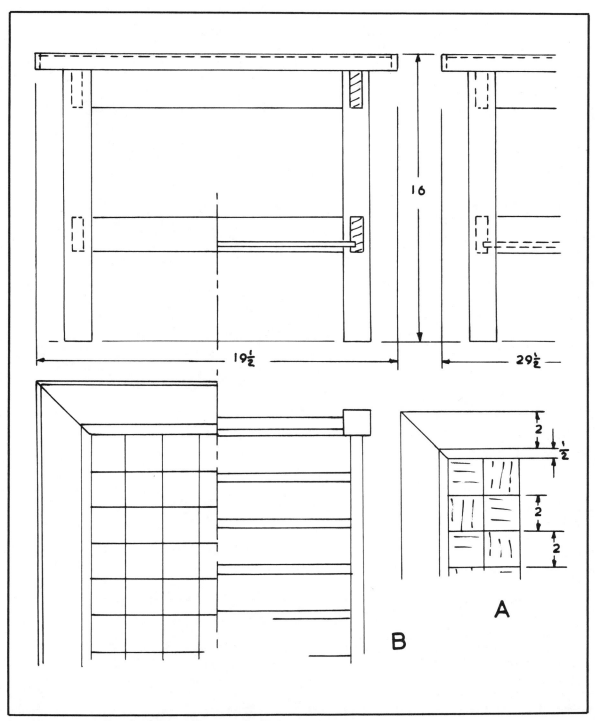

Fig. 4-2. Sizes and details of the checker-top magazine table.

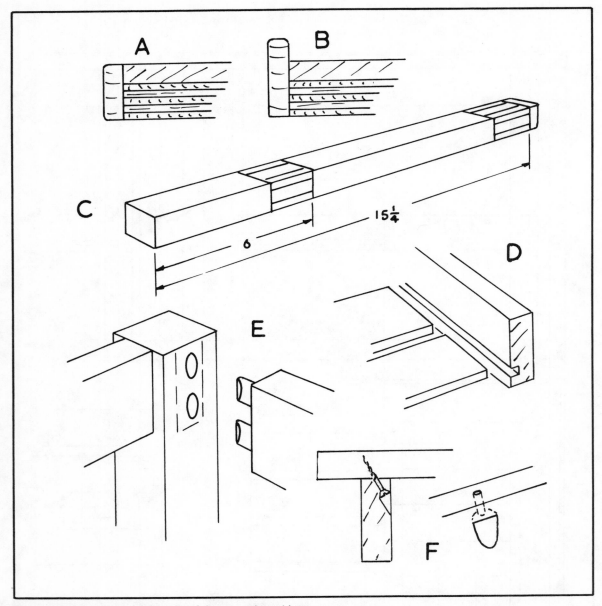

Fig. 4-3. Leg, top, and shelf details of the magazine table.

10. Drill all parts for dowels. Assemble the two end frames. Check that they match each other and are square.

11. Cut sufficient slats to length. As you assemble the lengthwise rails, fit in the slats evenly spaced. Put a little glue on the end of each slat to keep it in place. Square the framework while it is standing on a level surface. When the glue has set, cut the tops of the legs level with the rails. Invert the framework in position on the underside of the top and screw it on. Screws without glue should be sufficient.

Materials List for Checker-Top Magazine Table

84 squares	2 × 2 × ¼		2 edges	¼ × 1¼ × 30	
2 borders	2 × 30 × ¼		2 edges	¼ × 1¼ × 20	
2 borders	2 × 20 × ¼		4 legs	1½ × 1½ × 16	
2 borders	½ × 28 × ¼		4 rails	⅝ × 2 × 16	
2 borders	½ × 18 × ¼		4 rails	⅝ × 2 × 26	
1 top	19 × 30 × ½ plywood		10 slats	¼ × 2 × 18	

5

Display Shelves

A TABLE SAW CAN BE USED FOR CUTTING TENONS and is particularly useful, accurate, and speedy when large numbers of identical ones are needed, because the fences, stops, and guides can be set for each process in a long run of cuts.

This block of *display shelves* (Fig. 5-1) has identical mortise and tenon joints in all the supporting parts, so they can all be cut at the same time. The assembly may be made in almost any size, with any number of supports in a long block of shelves. Besides obvious display purposes, the shelves could serve as a bookcase or a room divider. All shelves need not be the same length, and the supports can be adjusted to suit.

The shelves may be solid wood, or they could be veneered particleboard. The supports should be made of an attractive hardwood if the shelves are intended as furniture in the home, but if the shelves are to be used in a store, shop, or garage, they can be straight-grained softwood, free from large knots, then painted.

The sample sizes (Fig. 5-2A) are for a block of shelves with the top one shorter, but the arrangement could be altered to suit needs or space. If prepared veneered particleboard is to be used for the shelves, get that first because it determines widths of the supports.

1. Have the shelf material ready. Square its ends and lightly chamfer or round any projecting corners. Prepare sufficient wood for all the parts of the framework, planed all round to the finished sizes.

2. Using the shelves as a guide, mark the lengths of the supports between shoulders (Fig. 5-3A). Allow for the lengths of the tenons and cut sufficient pieces to overall length (Fig. 5-3B).

3. The thickness of tenons should match the size mortises that can be cut with your drills, router bits, or chisels, but should be about one-third the thickness of the wood (Fig. 5-3C).

4. Prepare the lengthwise supports (Fig. 5-2B). They require the same tenons as the crosswise supports, but arranged horizontally (Fig. 5-3D). All tenons should go halfway through

Fig. 5-1. A block of shelves which may be used for display or as a room divider.

the mortised pieces. Cut all mortises.

5. Mark out the uprights (Fig. 5-2C and D). Cut the mortises to match the tenons.

6. Cut the mortises in the cross supports to match the tenons on the lengthwise supports. At the center frame, the mortises go right through, so the tenons meet, but at the end po-

sitions do not cut the mortises any deeper than necessary.

7. The tops of the uprights may be left square, but they will look better if shaped: *conical* (Fig. 5-3E), *chamfered* (Fig. 5-3F), or rounded (Fig. 5-3G).

8. Assemble the frames squarely and

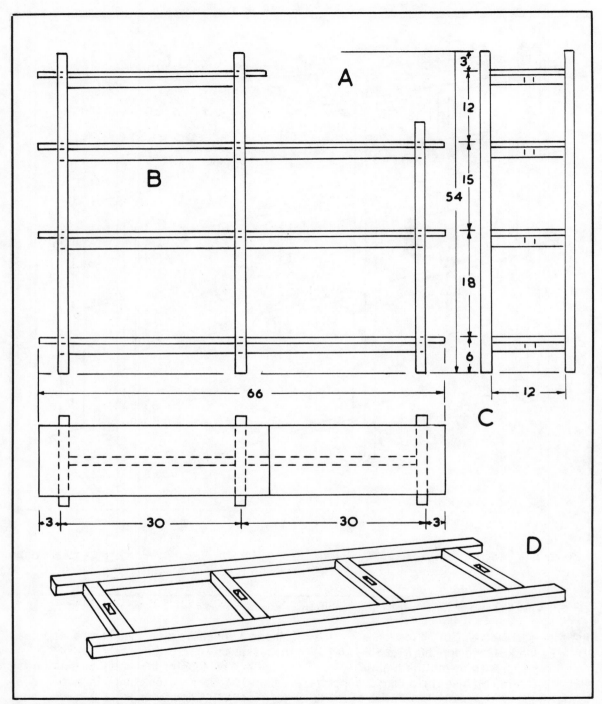

Fig. 5-2. Sizes and assembly details of the display shelves.

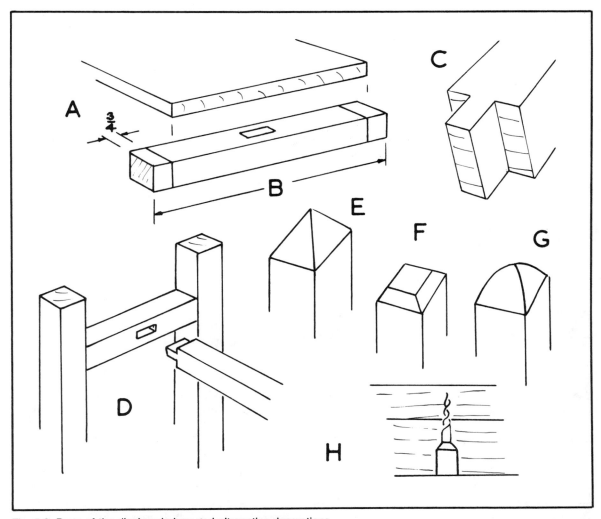

Fig. 5-3. Parts of the display shelves and alternative decorations.

without twist. See that they match each other. Join them with the lengthwise supports, while the parts are standing on a level surface. Compare diagonal measurements to see that the assembly is square. If necessary, clamp on a diagonal strut to hold the framework true while the glue sets.

9. It may be sufficient to merely rest the shelves in position, but they may be screwed from below. Unless you need to control warping, one screw near each end of a shelf should

be sufficient. You may *counterbore* to avoid the need for very long screws (Fig. 5-3H).

Materials List for Display Shelves

3 shelves	1	×	12	× 67
1 shelf	1	×	12	× 37
11 supports	1½	×	1½	× 15
4 uprights	1½	×	1½	× 55
2 uprights	1½	×	1½	× 44
7 supports	1½	×	1½	× 32

21

6

Kitchen Boards

DESPITE THE ADVENT OF PLASTICS FOR NEARLY everything, no enthusiastic cook will accept anything but wood for a surface on which to cut, chop, or roll. A professional chef has many boards which he looks after. Such a board could be just that—a simple flat piece of wood, however, there are many developments and variations that the user of a table saw can make. One attraction is the opportunity to use up oddments of wood that might otherwise be discarded.

Modern waterproof glues allow wood to be joined positively and with no need for complex jointing. Such joints will remain secure under wet conditions; something which could not be claimed for the glues of not so many years ago. Make sure the glue you obtain is described as *waterproof* and not just *water-resistant*. If it is suitable for boat building, you have the best.

Avoid resinous wood or those that are greasy or have an odor. A light color is more hygienic. A close grain is easier to clean and less likely to splinter. *Sycamore* is typical of the wood to choose. If you are laminating, you could use different woods for the sake of the resulting pattern, but beware of different hardnesses, which will result in an uneven surface after much use.

If you wish to use a single wide board, it is advisable for it to be *radially cut* from the log (Fig. 6-1A). You can check this by looking at the end grain lines, which will be fairly straight through the thickness (Fig. 6-1B). If you cut elsewhere from the log, the lines will be curved in varying degrees (Fig. 6-1C). If your wood gets wet, particularly more on one side than the other, as it may in kitchen use, it will warp. The effect is for grain lines to try to straighten. The radially cut board may get a little thicker, but it will remain flat (Fig. 6-1D). The board with curved lines will go out of shape (Fig. 6-1E).

A board may be held flat or given feet with *cleats* underneath (Fig. 6-2A). If the cleats are at the ends, there will be less risk of tipping (Fig. 6-2B). A further development is to make one cleat deeper with a notch, so it can be steadied over the edge of a table (Fig. 6-2C). Nailing or screwing are inadvisable, even if you use non-

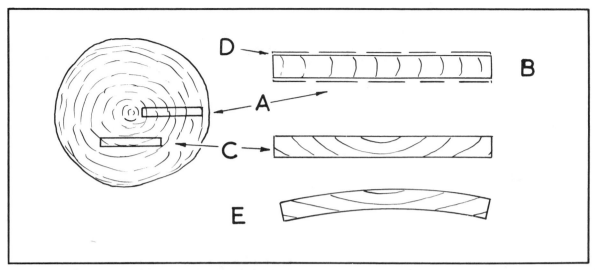

Fig. 6-1. How boards are affected when they dry out after being cut from a log.

corrosive fastenings. Glue between the surfaces may be sufficient, but a few dowels (Fig. 6-2D) will lock the parts together securely.

The risk of warping is removed if you *laminate* the wood by gluing strips together to make up the width (Fig. 6-2E). This is often described as *butcher block*, but the true butcher block uses end grain squares, as described later. For a laminated board, saw strips in random widths, then saw them all to the same thickness. Your board width may be made up of three or four pieces or a much larger number. It does not matter. Examine the end grain and alternate the grain lines as much as possible, then any tendency to warp will cancel out.

The board you are making is about ¾-inch thick and 10 inches square for chopping and cutting, or it could be 20 inches by 30 inches for rolling pastry. It is inadvisable to try to glue all the strips at the same time. It is easier to clamp and keep surfaces level if you first join strips in pairs and then bring pairs together after the first glue lines have set (Fig. 6-2F).

A board of lengthwise laminations should remain flat in use, but if you want to secure the board, or one made from a wide piece, and do not wish to put cleats underneath, there could be strips across the ends in the traditional pas-

try board manner. This involves cutting a *tongue* on the board ends, with a matching *groove* in the end pieces (Fig. 6-2G). Take the tongue into the other piece at least ½-inch, for stiffness. It will be easier to make the board finally finish level on both sides if the end pieces are slightly too thick at first, so you can plane and sand them level.

The true butcher block pattern is made of pieces of wood with their end grain on the surface (Fig. 6-3A). This provides the best long-lasting cutting surface. The board has to be made slightly thicker than the other boards—about 1-inch is satisfactory. The wood should be close-grained hardwood with little tendency to split.

Although it is possible to arrange a pattern with different sizes, it is advisable to make your first board from square stock all the same section. Suppose you have wood suitable for cutting to 1½-inch squares: a board 9 inches one way and 12 inches the other way would need 48 squares. At a final thickness of 1-inch, that means preparing a strip, or several oddments, totaling a length of 48 inches, with maybe a further 12 inches to allow for cutting. Start by gluing together pieces long enough to cut into eight blocks (Fig. 6-3B). These will make up the short

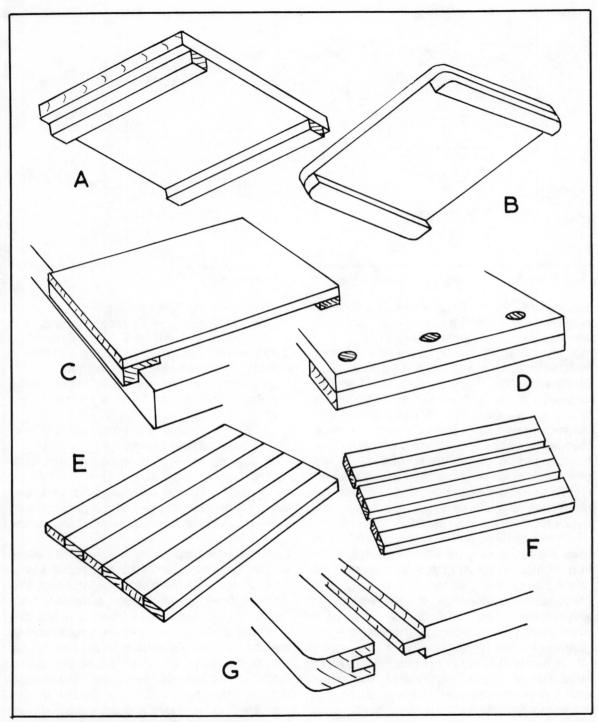

Fig. 6-2. A selection of boards for use in a kitchen.

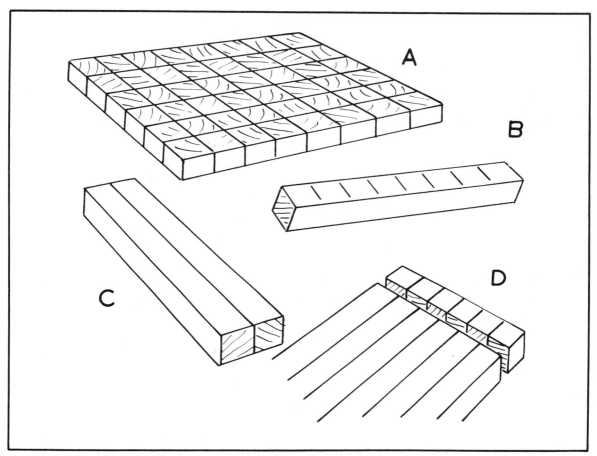

Fig. 6-3. Construction of butcher block boards.

way, so you need six strips, but it is safer to glue in pairs (Fig. 6-3C) before gluing the final joints.

Square one end. Remove surplus glue. True the surfaces flat, if necessary, but do not take off any more wood than you have to. Saw the block across into 1-inch pieces (Fig. 6-3D). Glue these pieces together, starting with pairs. When the glue has set, plane and sand the surfaces level, trim the edges, and round the corners.

Before use, it is advisable to soak the end grain butcher block in vegetable oil and repeat the treatment occasionally during its life. This reduces water absorption. Boards made in other ways may be treated in the same way, but side grain surfaces are not so absorbent.

There are many variations on the plain boards. A knife could be kept in one edge, if you recess for the handle and make a saw cut that is a push fit on the blade (Fig. 6-4A).

A handle could be provided. It might be turned with a dowel to fit into the edge of a board (Fig. 6-4B). A finger hole may be provided, either across one end or at the corner (Fig. 6-4C). Make it by drilling two ¾-inch holes at least 3 inches apart, then saw between and round the edges. Some kitchen boards that have survived from pioneer days have complicated decorative handles, but it is important to remember that any shaping of the board reduces the useful working area.

The oldtime grocer always cut cheese with

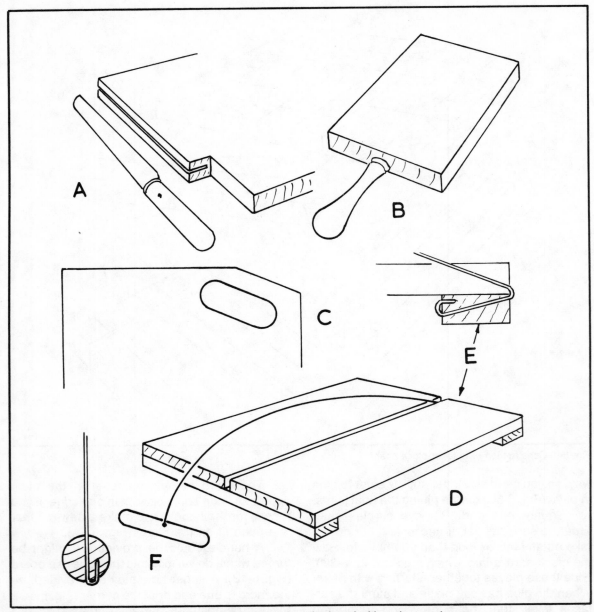

Fig. 6-4. A board with a slot for a knife, a handled board, and a board with a cheese wire.

a wire and not a knife. You can make a wire-cutting *cheeseboard* in two parts (Fig. 6-4D). Arrange a gap of about ⅛ inch. Use stainless steel wire, about 20-gauge. At one side, take it through a hole and turn its end over to drive into the wood (Fig. 6-4E). Allow a sufficient length to loop over the largest piece of cheese, then take the wire through a piece of ½-inch dowel rod 4 inches long (Fig. 6-4F). Position the board near the edge of a table, so you pull downwards over the edge as the wire cuts through the cheese.

7

Blanket Racks

A RACK WITH RAILS HAS MANY USES BESIDES holding blankets in a bedroom. Towels and other items may hang on a rack in a bathroom. Clothing may be dried or aired on a rack in a bathroom, laundry, or outdoors. Such a rack is fairly light, so it can be carried about and its function changed when required. Several variations are described (Fig. 7-1).

You can use dowel rods for rails, but squared strips with rounded corners are better for hanging, and they contribute to the strength of the assembly with their more rigid joints. For most racks, use ¾-inch-by-1½-inch hardwood or slightly thicker softwood, such as 1⅞-inch-by-⅞-inch, for all parts. You may use stouter square wood for the uprights of a very large rack.

These are racks in which nearly all the joints can be the same mortises and tenons, so it is possible to set up the table saw to make all the tenons in quantity.

1. For the simplest rack (Fig. 7-2A), prepare the wood for the rails with rounded corners

(Fig. 7-2B). The wood for the ends may be the same section, with sharpness taken off the angles.

2. Mark out the ends (Fig. 7-2C). Round or chamfer the tops.

3. Mark and cut the tenons on the rails and on the uprights. Cut mortises to match. Take the rail tenons through the ends for maximum strength, then plane level after assembly. The tenons at the feet may be about ¾-inch long.

4. Put blocks (Fig. 7-2D) under the feet and glue the feet squarely to the uprights. Glue the rails to the uprights and see that the rack stands upright.

5. For the second variation (Fig. 7-3A), construction is very similar, with the ends and main rails almost the same.

6. Cut *halving joints* for the spreaders (Fig. 7-3B).

7. On the two outer rails, cut the tenons across (Fig. 7-3C). Except for this, the joints are the same as the other rack.

8. If the rack would be better reduced in

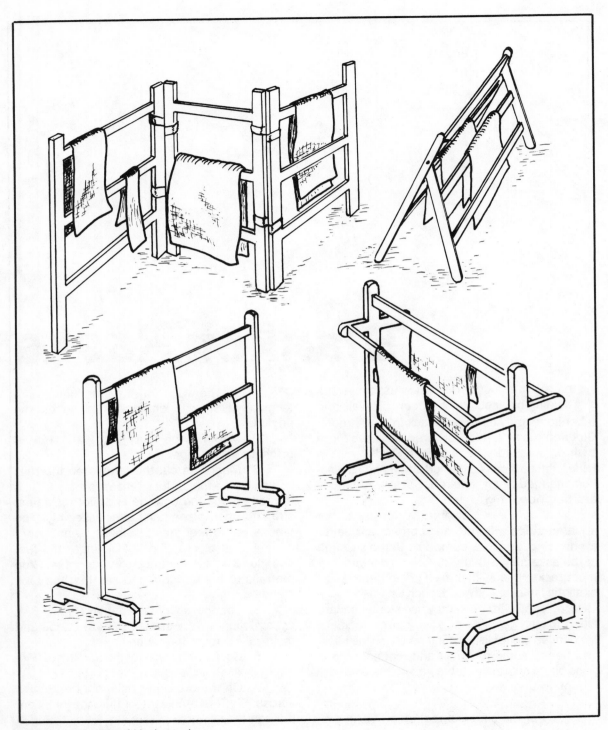

Fig. 7-1. A selection of blanket racks.

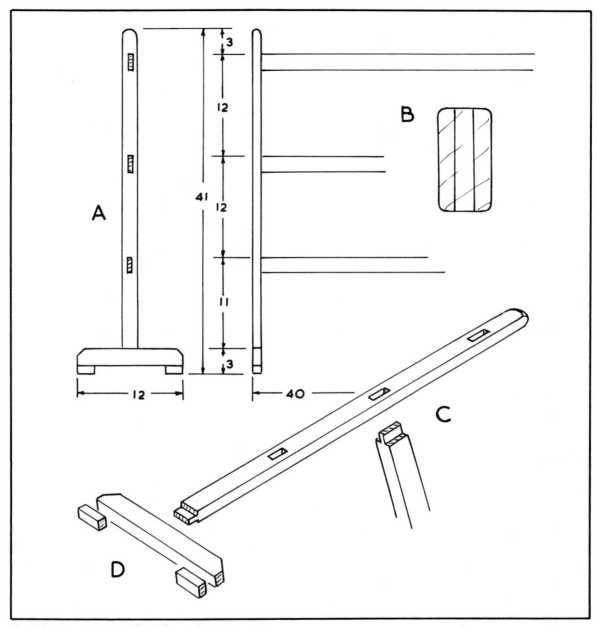

Fig. 7-2. Sizes and details of the first blanket rack.

size for storage, it can be made to fold (Fig. 7-4A). One side has three rails and the other pivots on it with two rails in the example shown, but the rack could be made larger and with a different number of rails.

9. Prepare wood for all parts and round the edges of rails, as in the other racks. All joints are the same mortises and tenons.

10. Mark out and cut the parts for the larger frame (Fig. 7-4B). Round the ends of the up-

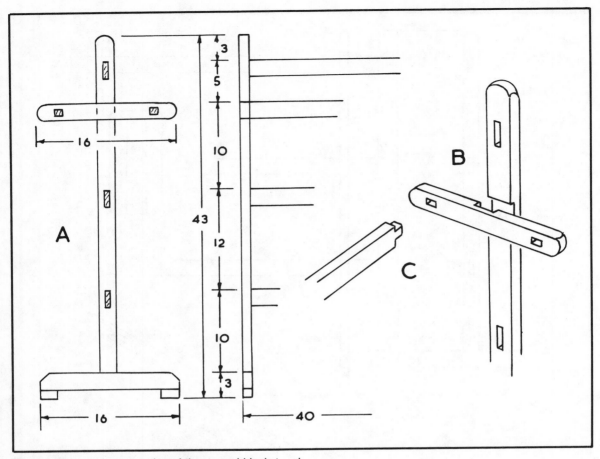

Fig. 7-3. Sizes and construction of the second blanket rack.

rights. Allow for the tenons going through the ends.

11. Make the inner frame (Fig. 7-4C) in a similar way, but the overall width must fit between the ends of the other part.

12. The pivots may be brass nuts and bolts (Fig. 7-4D), or dowels glued in the outer ends to extend through the other pieces (Fig. 7-4E).

13. If you want the rack to fold as compactly as possible, the inner frame ends may be notched (Fig. 7-4F), but do not cut away excessively, because that would weaken the wood. Marking the notches is best done during the trial assembly.

14. The fourth rack could be in two or three parts, which are all the same (Fig. 7-5A). The folding action allows them to stand firm, with the parts at angles to each other, or to fold flat.

15. Construction is straightforward, with tenons going about 1 inch into the legs (Fig. 7-5B).

16. It is possible to use ordinary metal hinges between the parts, but that would only allow folding one way.

17. The traditional method of hinging this type of rack is with strips of stout tape, upholstery webbing, or pieces of leather (real or a plastic substitute).

18. It may be advisable to try hinging two pieces of scrap wood first. Center the tape on

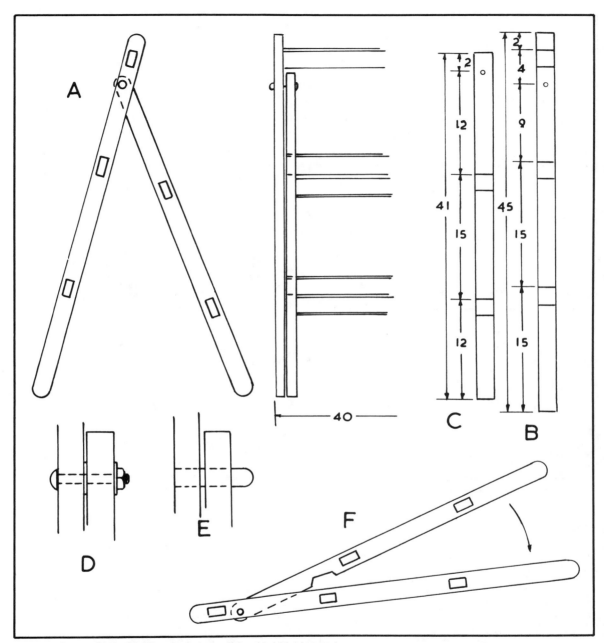

Fig. 7-4. The method of folding and sizes of the third blanket rack.

one piece and tack it to the inner edge of the wood. Cross the ends around the wood and onto the other piece, then tack there (Fig. 7-5C). If you are using fabric, turn under the ends to prevent fraying. Keep the crossings close and pull the tape tight. Arrange these hinges near the top and bottom, and you will be able to fold the parts either way.

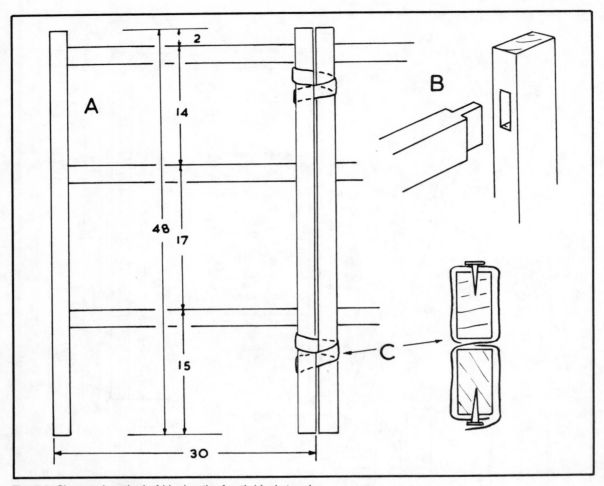

Fig. 7-5. Sizes and method of hinging the fourth blanket rack.

Materials List for Blanket Racks

First Rack

2 ends	¾ × 1½ × 42
2 feet	¾ × 1½ × 13
3 rails	¾ × 1½ × 41

Second Rack

2 ends	¾ × 1½ × 43
2 feet	¾ × 1½ × 17
2 crossbars	¾ × 1½ × 17
5 rails	¾ × 1½ × 41

Third Rack

2 ends	¾ × 1½ × 46
2 ends	¾ × 1½ × 42
5 rails	¾ × 1½ × 41

Fourth Rack

| 6 uprights | ¾ × 1½ × 49 |
| 9 rails | ¾ × 1½ × 30 |

8

Paneled Chest

MANY MEDIEVAL CHESTS WERE PANELED, BE-cause that produced a lighter construction than using solid boards, and it allowed wood to be used without the need of joints to make up widths when the glues available could not be trusted.

We do not have those problems, but paneled construction is still attractive. Such a chest made with solid wood framing and plywood panels is an interesting project. If polished hardwood is used, the chest could become a blanket box or other storage item in the home, where it would be an attractive piece of furniture. The suggested chest (Figs. 8-1 and 8-2) is a suitable height for seating. With a fitted cushion, it can double as a window seat. With a painted finish, the chest could be used in the workshop, garage, or garden shed for storage and seating.

This chest has ¾-inch-by-3-inch section framing and ¼-inch plywood panels. Construction is based on framed units, which are doweled together. The bottom is an inset piece of plywood. All parts are glued and there will be very little need for nails or screws.

1. Prepare sufficient pieces of wood with grooves ½-inch deep to suit the plywood (Fig. 8-2A). The center pieces of top, front, and back need grooves both sides (Fig. 8-2B).

2. Make the front and back first. Cut tenons to fit in the grooves (Fig. 8-3A). Cut the plywood panels a little undersize so the tenon joints can be pulled tight without being stopped by plywood touching the bottoms of the grooves. Assemble with adequate glue on the tenons, but apply it sparingly at the edges of the panels. See that the back and front are square and match each other.

3. The ends fit between the back and front frames (Fig. 8-2C and 3B). Make the ends and drill the corners for ⅜-inch dowels (Fig. 8-2D) at about 3-inch intervals (Fig. 8-3C).

4. Put strips around the bottom edges of the frames to support the chest bottom (Fig. 8-2E). Cut the bottom plywood close to size, so

Fig. 8-1. This chest is made of framed plywood panels.

it is ready to put in when you start assembly.

5. Join back and front to the ends and fit in the bottom with glue and a few screws.

6. Make the top in a similar way to the front. It should be level with the back, but overlap at the front and ends by 1 inch (Fig. 8-2F).

7. Use three 3-inch hinges, with one at the center and the others a few inches in from the

ends. Let them into the top and the edge of the back (Fig. 8-2G), but leave a little clearance so the lid will close without straining the hinges.

8. There is no need for a handle or fastener for normal use. It may be advisable to fit a folding strut at one end or use a cord between screw eyes, to prevent the lid falling too far back.

34

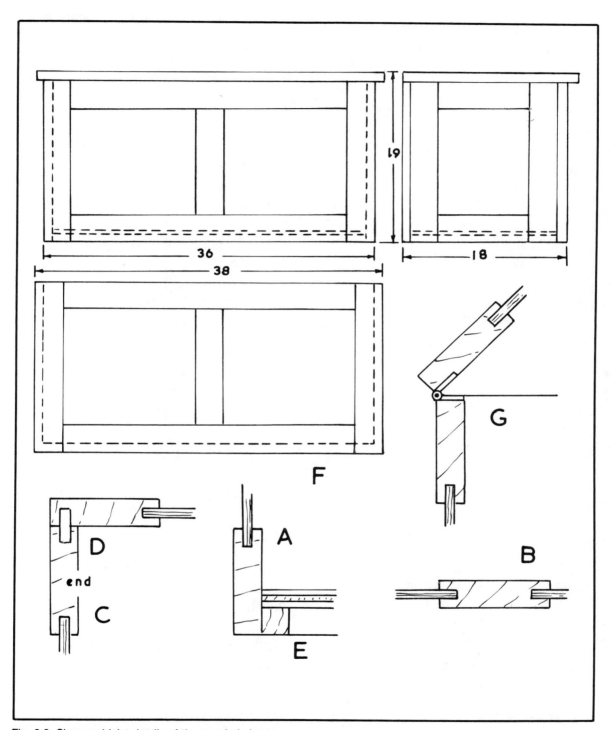

Fig. 8-2. Sizes and joint details of the paneled chest.

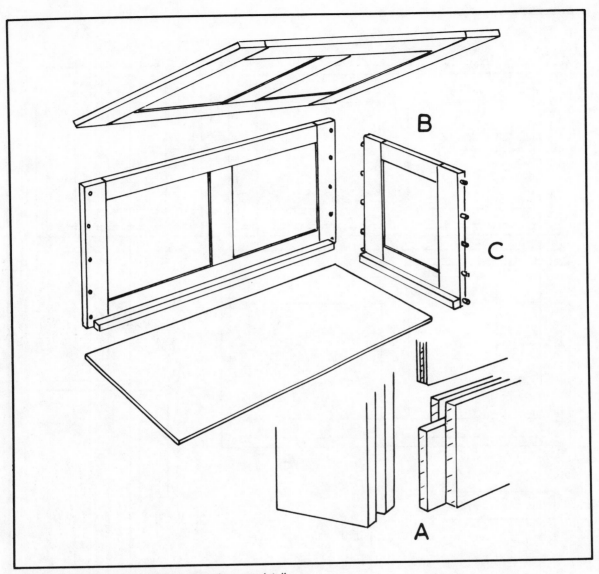

Fig. 8-3. The parts of a paneled chest and corner details.

Materials List for Paneled Chest

8 upright frames	¾ × 3 × 19	2 bottom strips	¾ × ¾ × 36		
2 upright frames	¾ × 3 × 17	2 bottom strips	¾ × ¾ × 18		
4 long frames	¾ × 3 × 35	1 bottom	16 × 36 × ½ plywood		
4 end frames	¾ × 3 × 15	4 panels	14 × 15 × ¼ plywood		
2 top frames	¾ × 3 × 40	2 panels	12 × 15 × ¼ plywood		
2 top frames	¾ × 3 × 20	2 top panels	15 × 16 × ¼ plywood		
1 top frame	¾ × 3 × 17				

9

Carry-All

ONE THING A TABLE SAW DOES WELL IS CUT ANY number of pieces of wood to the same size. If the project does not require long pieces, they can be cut from oddments that might otherwise be discarded. This carry-all (Fig. 9-1) could be used for magazines, knitting or sewing items, or anything you may wish to keep together and carry about. The sides are made up of vertical strips like a small version of a paling fence.

The parts should be furniture-quality hardwood, but the pales need not be the same wood as the other parts. They are effective if in a contrasting darker or lighter color. The pales are held in place with screws, which form part of the decorative design and may be roundhead brass or plated finish.

1. Select wood for the pales. They are shown ¼-inch-by-1-inch finished section and could be cut through from a 1-inch board or brought to size both ways from oddments. If it would be more convenient to cut your wood to another section, that does not matter, but the

Fig. 9-1. This carry-all for magazines or other contents has paling sides.

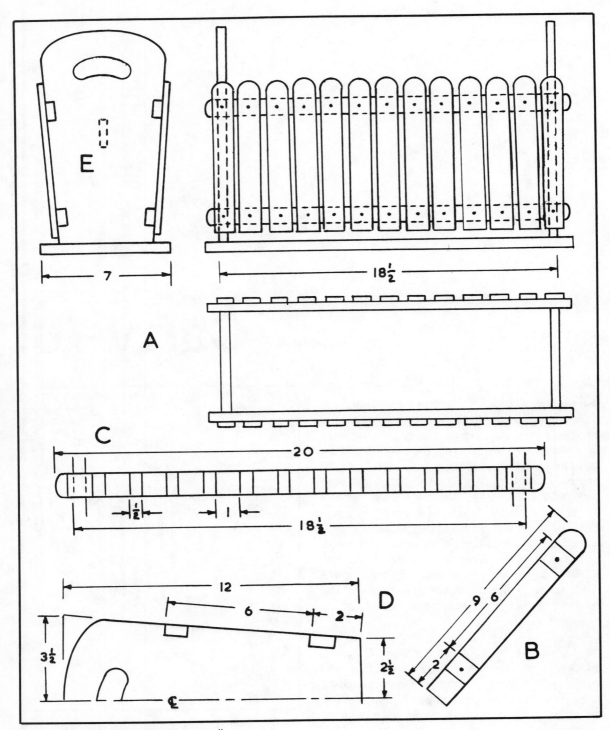

Fig. 9-2. Suggested sizes for the carry-all.

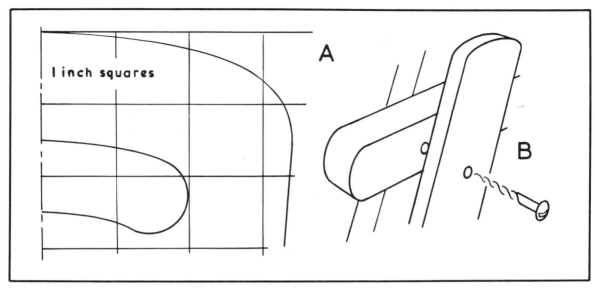

Fig. 9-3. The end shape and assembly details for the carry-all.

sizes of other parts may have to be adjusted to give an even spacing (Fig. 9-2A).

2. Make sufficient pales, planed and sanded, with rounded tops and the screw hole positions marked (Fig. 9-2B).

3. Mark out the four rails (Fig. 9-2C). They go through the ends and extend a little, so the end pales overlap the trough ends and are screwed through to hold the rails as well.

4. Mark out the pair of ends (Figs. 9-2D and 9-3A). Cut notches for the rails. Shape the tops and the hand holes and well round their edges.

5. Make the bottom to overlap the other parts. Round its edges and drill it for screwing on.

6. Join the pales to the rails squarely, leaving the end ones to be added when you join to the ends. See that the assembly is square and screw on the bottom. Use glue in the joints and

make the end screws through the pales the same diameter as the others, but long enough to hold in the trough ends (Fig. 9-3B).

7. It may be satisfactory to leave the underside bare. Much depends on where the carry-all will be used. Four rubber feet can be screwed on or the bottom covered with cloth.

8. The carry-all is described without anything built inside, but if magazines are to be stood on edge, a central rail (Fig. 9-2E) prevents them falling over if the carry-all is only partially filled.

Materials List for Carry-All

2 ends	$\frac{5}{8}$	× 7 × 13
4 rails	$\frac{1}{2}$	× 1 × 21
26 pales	$\frac{1}{4}$	× 1 × 10
1 bottom	$\frac{5}{8}$	× 7 × 22

10

Dresser Stool

A STOOL FOR USE IN FRONT OF A DRESSER OR MIRror is a welcome piece of furniture in a bedroom. It also provides an extra seat for other purposes. A similar seat forms a piano stool. An upholstered top increases comfort and is easy to make with modern materials. The height of the stool can be altered to suit the purpose. This stool (Fig. 10-1) is shown at a height that will probably suit your dresser (Fig. 10-2A). For a piano it may have to be 2 or 3 inches higher.

A furniture-quality hardwood should be used. It is possible to use mortise and tenon joints, but dowels are shown. The upholstered top is made as a separate unit, and it lifts out.

1. Start by preparing all the parts that finish 1¼-inch thick. Most are 2½ inches wide. Cut rabbets in the two top rails (Fig. 10-2B).

2. Mark out the legs (Fig. 10-3A). Make the rails that go between them and assemble the two end frames with two or three ⅝-inch dowels in each joint (Fig. 10-3B). There may be slots to form hand grips under the top pieces (Fig. 10-3C). Round the outer corners.

3. Fit the lengthwise rails between the end frames (Fig. 10-2D).

4. Square the assembly in all directions while it is standing on a level surface.

5. Fit the strips across the ends level with the rabbets (Fig. 10-2C).

6. Make the frame for the upholstered top with doweled corners (Fig. 10-3D). The central panel may be a piece of ½-inch plywood set into rabbets (Fig. 10-3E), or it could be fillets inside the frame (Fig. 10-3F). The frame has to fit reasonably tightly into the stool after it has been upholstered, so the thickness of its covering cloth must be allowed for. The outer edges may be planed after you have experimented with the covering. Chamfer the edges slightly. Drill a few holes in the plywood so air can move in and out of the padding as it compresses and expands.

7. The padding of the seat may be rubber or plastic foam about 1½ inches thick. Over this goes a piece of woven cloth or some plastic-coated fabric. Choose a reasonably flexible ma-

Fig. 10-1. This stool with an upholstered top is particularly suitable for use with a dresser.

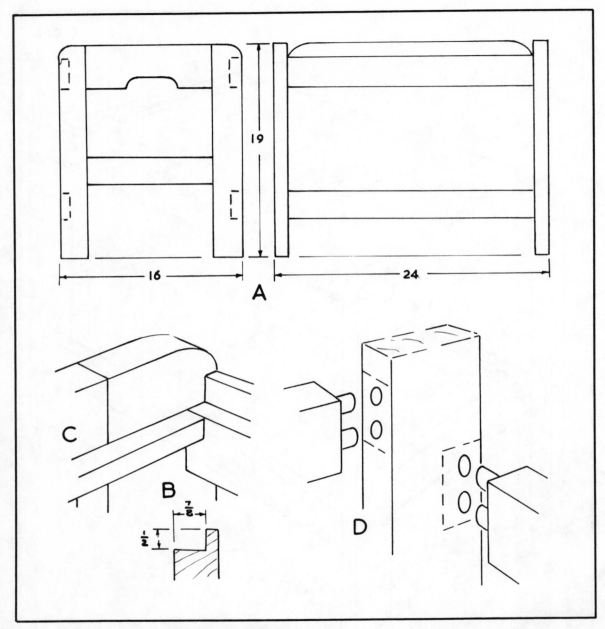

Fig. 10-2. Sizes and construction details of the dresser stool.

terial. If you wish to cover with a light fabric to match other furnishings, the foam should first be covered with plain cloth. With heavier fabric, there is no need for this. Fix it with tacks, ⅜-inch or ½-inch long.

8. Cut the block of foam about ¼ inch too big all round and bevel the lower edges (Fig. 10-3G). This allows for compression and for a rounded edge.

9. Stretch the covering material over the

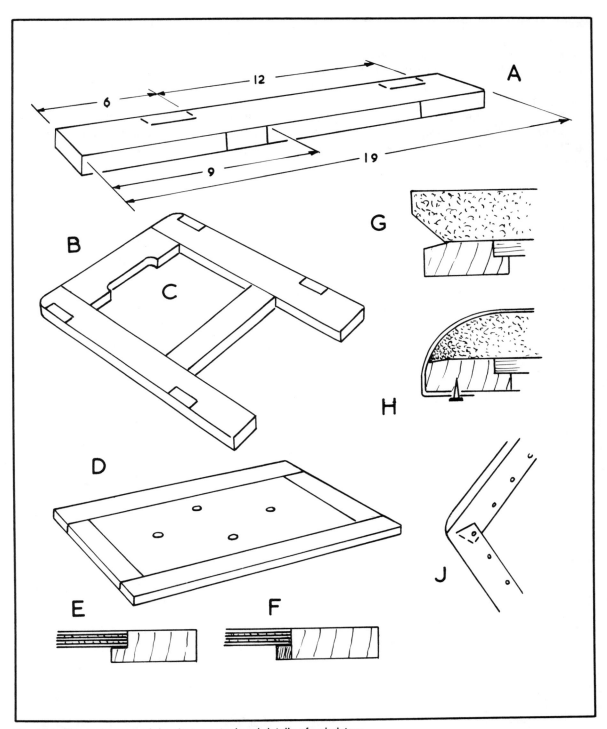

Fig. 10-3. The main parts of the dresser stool and details of upholstery.

foam and start tacking near the center of opposite sides (Fig. 10-3H). Do the same at the centers the other way. Work outwards towards the corners. What tack spacing you use to get an even tension depends on the materials, but 1½ inches will probably be about right.

10. At the corners, pull diagonally to get a good shape on top and notch the cloth underneath to allow tacking without bulk (Fig. 10-3J). Trim the cloth neatly inside the lines of tacks.

Materials List for Dresser Stool

4 legs	1¼	×	2½	×	20	
2 rails	1¼	×	2½	×	13	
4 rails	1¼	×	2½	×	24	
2 rails	1¼	×	4	×	13	
2 strips	¾	×	¾	×	16	
2 tops	1	×	2½	×	23	
2 tops	1	×	2½	×	15	
1 top	16	×	23	×	½	plywood

11

Stacking Trays

IF YOU HAVE A *COMB JOINT ATTACHMENT* FOR YOUR table saw, the making of boxes and trays is simple, and the results are strong. It is easy to make any number of identical trays, which can be mounted in a stand like a block of drawers. This arrangement is useful for storage in a shop, or for sorting papers and keeping them tidy on a desk. Anyone with a hobby that involves many odds and ends can keep them sorted and ready for use.

This *block of trays* (Fig. 11-1) could be made in any number, or it would be possible to use the idea for a stack of trays side by side, so the assembly is wide, rather than high. The example is a simple stack of three matching trays (Fig. 11-2). A close-grained hardwood is best, as it will look good, and the risk of wood breaking out during cutting is minimal. The wood may be painted, but the stack may be given a smart appearance by varnishing or polishing. Sizes may have to be adjusted to suit your finger jointing equipment, but the trays are shown made with ⅜-inch thick wood and combs or fingers cut ⅜-inch

wide. Tray bottoms may be ⅛-inch hardboard or plywood.

1. Prepare the wood for the tray sides and ends. Groove the sides and front pieces to half thickness for the bottom (Fig. 11-3A). Cut the back to fit above the bottom, so the bottom may be slid in after the other parts have been assembled.

2. Cut the comb joints and hollow the fronts (Fig. 11-3B).

3. Assemble all trays. Slide in the bottoms and drive screws upwards into the backs (Fig. 11-3C). When the glue has set, plane off any excess wood, round edges, and sand surfaces.

4. Cut strips for the runners and make them up as long as the trays and with enough extra length for a stop across at the back (Fig. 11-3D).

5. Although the posts could be merely glued and screwed to the runners, they will be more positively located if you notch them to about half thickness on the guides (Fig. 11-3E).

Fig. 11-1. A stacking tray unit for use in the office, shop, or home.

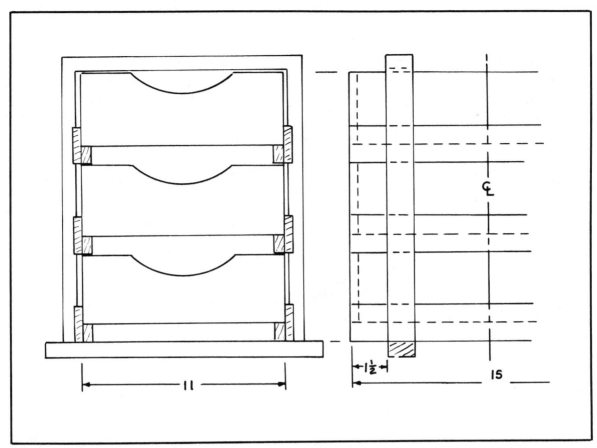

Fig. 11-2. Sizes of the stacking trays.

6. The tray stops will also act as spacers at the back, but to keep the posts the correct distance apart, join strips across at their tops, also with comb joints (Fig. 11-3F).

7. Put strips across to form feet (Fig. 11-3G) with dowels, or mortise and tenon joints to the posts.

8. All joints should be glued, but round-head brass or plated screws will give the stack of trays a functional and workmanlike appearance.

9. A bar joining the centers of the top crossing pieces can form a handle for carrying the stack.

Materials List for Stacking Trays

6 tray sides	⅜	×	5	×	16
3 tray fronts	⅜	×	5	×	12
3 tray backs	⅜	×	4½	×	12
3 tray bottoms	11	×	16	×	⅛
		hardboard			
6 runners	½	×	1	×	17
6 runners	½	×	2	×	17
3 stops	½	×	1	×	12
4 posts	¾	×	1½	×	25
2 tops	¾	×	1½	×	14
2 feet	¾	×	1½	×	16

47

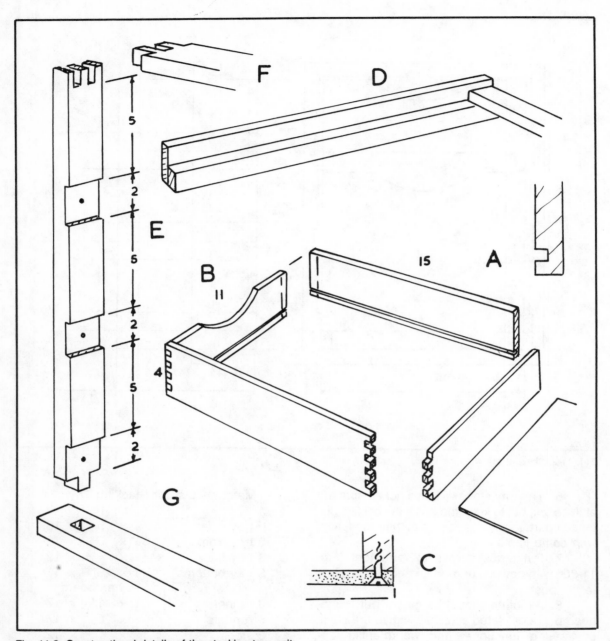

Fig. 11-3. Constructional details of the stacking tray unit.

12

Classic Table

WHAT MAY BE REGARDED AS THE CLASSIC TYPE of table has tapered legs without lower rails. Rigidity comes from the joints between the legs and the top rails, which must be fairly deep to give adequate width in the joints. The top overlaps and has molded edges (Fig. 12-1).

A table saw will cut the tapered legs, either by following a line or, preferably, with the aid of a *wedge-shaped jig* or *push stick,* which keeps the wood at the correct angle to the fence. This may be cut for the particular job or, if you expect to cut tapers frequently, you could make an adjustable guide.

The wood should be a good hardwood that will have an attractive grain when polished. Joints between rails and legs may be dowels, but if you want to follow tradition in this table, use mortises and tenons, which are described in these instructions. The top is held on with *buttons,* in the traditional way, to allow for expansion and contraction without the risk of the top splitting. The sizes shown (Fig. 12-2) are for a

light side table, but the method of construction could be used for tables of other sizes.

1. Mark out the legs (Fig. 12-2A) before cutting the tapers. Leave a little extra wood at the tops for trimming level after the framework is assembled.

2. Cut the rails to size. Make grooves near the tops of the inner surfaces (Fig. 12-2B) to take the buttons. Mark and cut the joints between the rails and the legs (Fig. 12-3A). To get maximum glue area, take the tenons in to meet and miter their ends (Fig. 12-2C).

3. Cut the tapers on the legs. They go from the full 1¾ inches square below the rail positions to 1-inch square at the foot. Follow sawing with planing. If the saw leaves a reasonably smooth surface, light hand planing will be better than using a power plane.

4. Sand the wood. Take sharpness off the lower edges of the rails. They may be molded.

5. Assemble the long sides. Because

Fig. 12-1. A classic table for use in the home.

there will be no lower framing to hold the assembly true, careful squaring is important. Check also for lack of twist.

6. Assemble the rails the other way, again checking squareness. Compare diagonal measurements across the tops of the legs, for squareness that way.

7. Make the top by gluing sufficient boards (Fig. 12-3B). The final size should overhang the legs by about 1½ inches all around.

8. The edges may be left square, be rounded (Fig. 12-3C), or be molded (Fig. 12-3D and E).

9. Make buttons. On the size table suggested, two in each side towards the legs should be sufficient (Fig. 12-3F). Make each so that when it is screwed to the top, its projecting tongue will pull up on the groove (Fig. 12-3G).

10. Invert the framework on the underside of the top and locate it centrally. When you screw the buttons, allow clearance so any movement of the top is not restricted.

11. See that the table stands level. If necessary, adjust the bottoms of legs. Take sharpness off them, so as not to mark carpets.

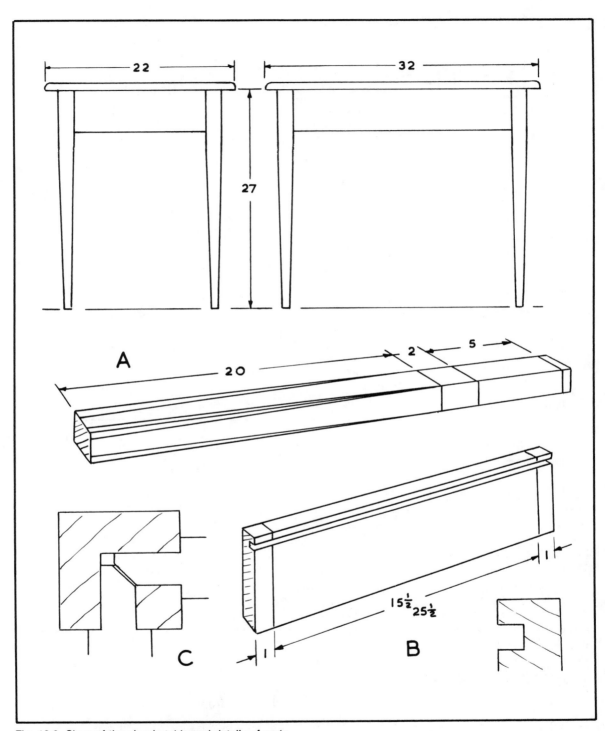

Fig. 12-2. Sizes of the classic table and details of parts.

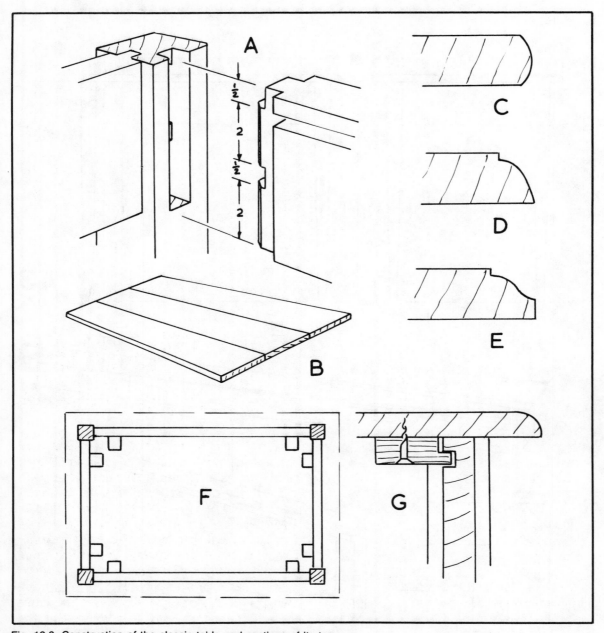

Fig. 12-3. Construction of the classic table and sections of its top.

Materials List for Classic Table

4 legs	1¾ × 1¾ × 28	Buttons from	¾ × 1½ × 24
2 rails	⅞ × 5 × 29	1 top	¾ × 22 × 33 joined
2 rails	⅞ × 5 × 19		boards

13

Wall Tables

FLOOR SPACE IS OFTEN LIMITED, AND A TABLE OUT of use may occupy more space than you wish to spare. Folding tables may be the answer, but another way of providing table space when needed, but avoiding the use of much floor space at other times, is to attach a table to the wall, either pivoting so it can be swung down out of the way or removable so it will fold its leg flat, and can be stored elsewhere.

Examples of both types are described in this project (Fig. 13-1). The tables can be made as good-quality furniture, for use in a hallway or any room, or they could have a more utilitarian construction and finish, for use in a shop or garage. The first is made of hardwood and polished, while the second could include softwoods and plywood and be finished with paint.

The usual height of a table is about 30 inches. A flat top that swings down cannot project more than this from the wall if it is to clear the floor, but a lift-off table may project any reasonable amount. It could be large enough to serve as a dining table (Fig. 13-2) or may be little more than a ledge.

1. The lift-off table may have a solid wood top, but it is shown with framed plywood covered with Formica or similar plastic and edged with a solid strip (Fig. 13-3A). The framing underneath has ¾-inch-by-1½-inch strips at the sides, a 3-inch wide piece at the wall end, and a piece 6 inches wide to take the hinged leg at the outer end (Figs. 13-3B and 13-2A). The narrow strips are cut into the 6-inch piece and mitered.

2. Glue and pin the plywood to its framing, glue on the Formica, then level the edges to take the border, which is mitered at the corners.

3. At the wall end, the table top hooks into a slotted piece attached to the wall (Fig. 13-2B). Fit a strip across the full width of the table end (Fig. 13-3C).

4. Make the wall assembly with a plywood back, through which screws may go into the wall.

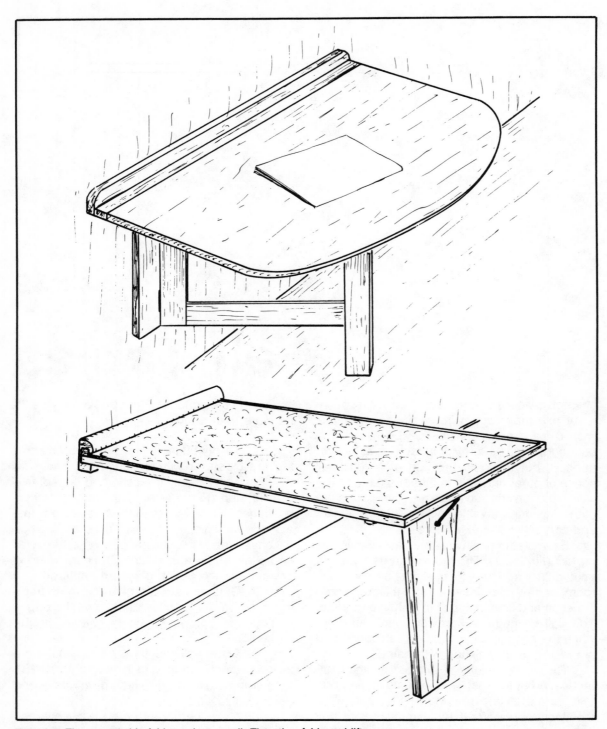

Fig. 13-1. The upper table folds against a wall. The other folds and lifts away.

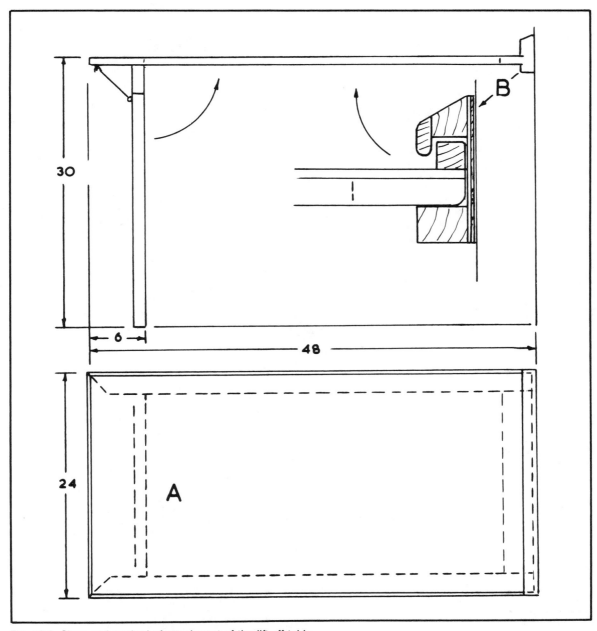

Fig. 13-2. Sizes and method of attachment of the lift-off table.

Arrange enough clearance for the table to be hooked in while held in a tilted-up position. Round the lower edge of the table enough to allow easy entry.

5. The leg is T-shaped, with a mortise and tenon joint between the parts (Fig. 13-3D). Taper the leg to the floor and round the outer corners.

6. Position the leg so two hinges may be fitted to the edge of the wide board, but make

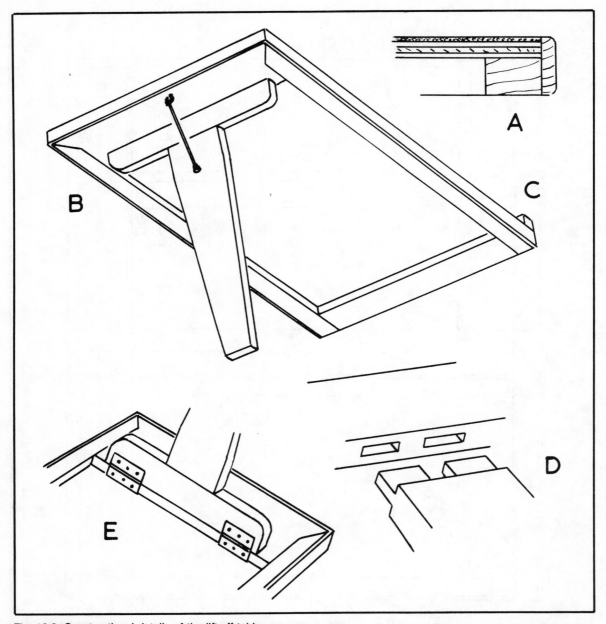

Fig. 13-3. Constructional details of the lift-off table.

sure the leg top bears against the wood above, and the load is not taken only by the hinge knuckles (Fig. 13-3E).

7. Use a hook (at least 6 inches long) and an eye to keep the leg vertical when the table is in use.

8. The flap table is described with a solid wood top having an elliptical edge (Fig. 13-4), but the top could be any other shape or built up in a similar way to the other table.

9. Make the table top by joining several boards to make up the width. Cut its outline and

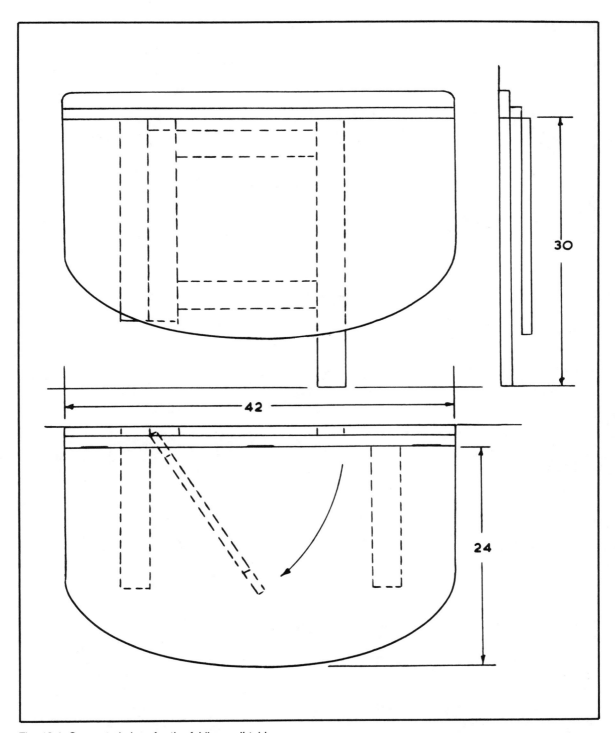

Fig. 13-4. Suggested sizes for the folding wall table.

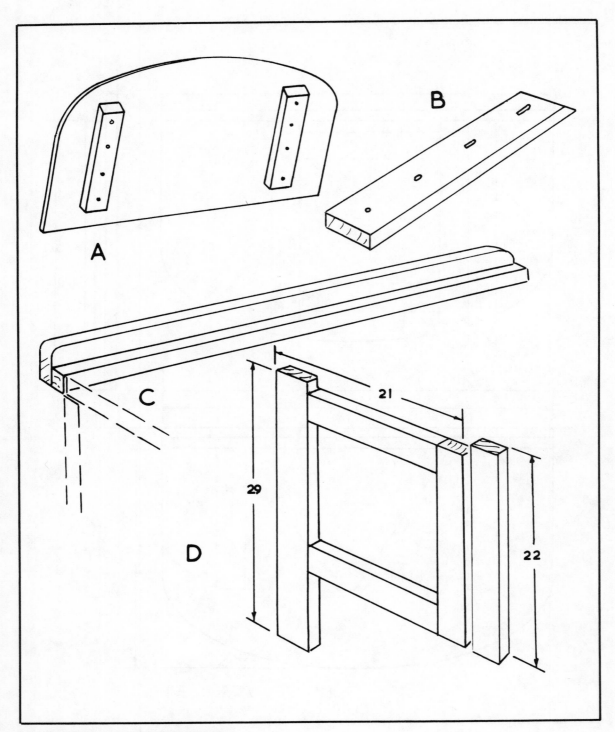

Fig. 13-5. The parts of a folding wall table.

round or mold the edges.

10. If you expect there may be a risk of warping, screw two *battens* underneath (Fig. 13-5A). Put them far enough apart to clear the gate leg. To allow for expansion and contraction, put the screw nearest the wall through a round hole, but put others through slots (Fig. 13-5B) so the screws can move with the top.

11. Make a strip as long as the table to screw to the wall and put a piece on it to hold the top clear of the parts underneath when it is folded down (Fig. 13-5C).

12. A *gate leg* is used so the table will be supported from the floor, which is more rigid than using a bracket from the wall only.

13. Make the leg a suitable height to hold the top level. Join the parts (Fig. 13-5D) with dowels or mortise and tenon joints.

14. Hinge the gate leg to a vertical piece screwed to the wall in a position that brings the leg assembly central when folded back.

15. The number of hinges you use for the top depends on the length, but one 2-inch or 3-inch hinge near each end and one or two spaced evenly between them should be satisfactory.

16. When the leg is pulled out to support the top it should be positioned central in the length of the top. Experiment to get the best place and put a small block under the top to act as a stop.

Materials List for Wall Tables

Lift-Off Table

1 top	24	× 48	× ½ plywood	
2 top frames	¾	× 1½	× 49	
1 top frame	¾	× 3	× 24	
1 top frame	¾	× 6	× 24	
2 top borders	⅜	× 1¼	× 49	
2 top boarders	⅜	× 1¼	× 25	
1 wall hook	¾	× ¾	× 25	
1 leg	1¼	× 5	× 29	
1 leg top	1¼	× 3	× 20	
1 wall support	4	× 25	× ½ plywood	
1 wall support	1¼	× 1¼	× 25	
1 wall support	⅞	× 1¼	× 25	
1 wall support	⅜	× 1	× 25	

Flap Table

1 top	⅞	× 24	× 43 joined boards	
1 back	⅞	× 3	× 43	
1 back	⅞	× ⅞	× 43	
2 battens	⅞	× 3	× 16	
4 gate legs	⅞	× 3	× 22	
1 gate leg	⅞	× 3	× 31	

14

Yard Seat

PORTABLE AND FOLDING SEATS HAVE THEIR USES outdoors, but it is convenient to have more permanent seating which can be left outside almost indefinitely. Such a seat could be for one person, or it may be long enough for two or more. The method of construction is almost the same. If the seat is to stand up to all kinds of weather, it has to be fairly rugged and securely constructed from substantial parts. It cannot include upholstery or canvas, so any concession to comfort has to come from its shaping and the addition of cushions, which are stored under shelter.

This project is shown as a *two-seat bench* (Fig. 14-1), but it could be reduced to half length as a single seat and the diagonal struts left out. The legs are 3-inch square section, and the other parts are 1-inch-by-3-inches, so all the wood may be cut from larger sections with two settings of the table saw. If sufficient wood is prepared in advance, construction can be quite rapid. For anyone wishing to make items for sale, these benches can be tackled as quantity production,

with the individual processes done for all benches in the run at the same time.

The seat may be made from softwood and protected with paint. A durable hardwood might be left untreated or given a coat of oil. Any wood may be treated with preservative. Oils and preservatives may take some time to fully dry, so do not risk marking clothing by using the seat too soon.

Joints should be made with waterproof glue and screws, but many are also notched. The notches provide accurate locations and take most of the loads in use. Use the actual pieces of wood as guides to notch sizes, so you get close fits. The drawing (Fig. 14-2A) shows many parts crossing squarely, but the seat is given a slight slope and the back is raked to match it. Set out the main lines of an end first (Fig. 14-3A) to obtain the angles of notches in the legs.

1. Make the pair of back legs (Fig. 14-2B). All notches may be ½-inch deep. The slope for the back should hold the slats about square to

Fig. 14-1. This yard seat is intended for two people.

the seat.

2. Make the pair of front legs (Fig. 14-2C). At the top, allow for a tenon 1-inch wide and ½-inch long to go into the armrest.

3. The bottom rail (Fig. 14-2D) fits into the legs grooves without notching, so it projects ½ inch.

4. The seat rail fits into the leg grooves in the same way. Get its length and angle from your setting out. At the front, it projects 1 inch from the leg and is notched to take the front support (Figs. 14-2E and 14-3B).

5. Make the arms to fit into the rear leg notches and extend 2 inches ahead of the front leg (Figs. 14-2F and 14-3C). Cut mortises ½-inch deep to suit the tenons on the legs. It may be satisfactory to merely glue the joints, but you can get extra strength from *fox wedging* (Fig. 14-3D). Make saw cuts across the tenons, then use short wedges in them, so when you force the joints together the wedges hit the bottom of the mortise and spread the tenon.

6. Round all exposed edges. Assemble the pair of ends. Screws are driven so the heads are on the surface, although it will be neater to counterbore them and glue in plugs (Fig. 14-3E).

61

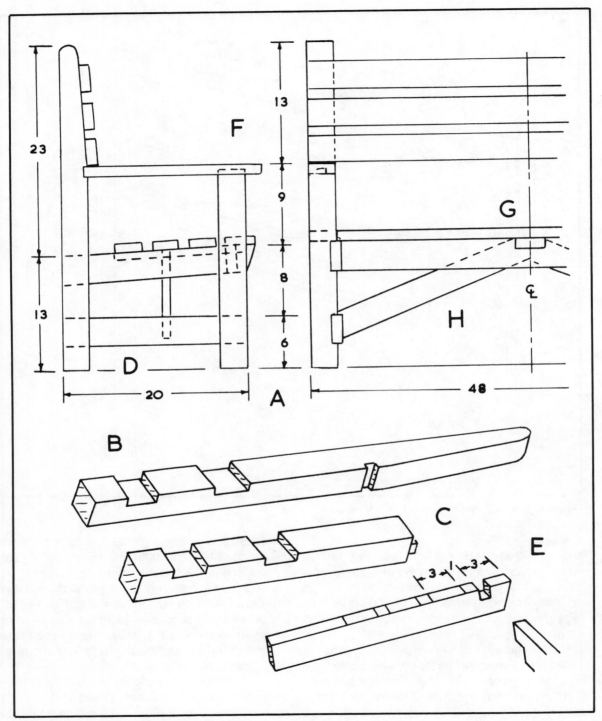

Fig. 14-2. Sizes and parts of the yard seat.

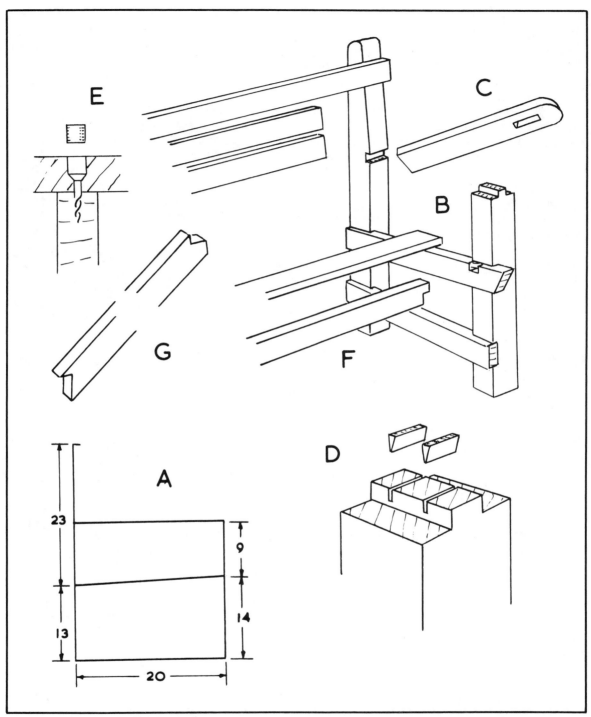

Fig. 14-3. Assembly details of the yard seat.

7. The back and seat slats are all the same. Let them reach the outside lines of the legs and glue and screw them in place. Notch the front slat around the legs. Include the support under the front seat slat (Fig. 14-3F), with glue and a few screws in the length.

8. Join the seat slats with a stiffener across under the center (Fig. 14-2G).

9. Make diagonal struts (Fig. 14-2H), notched over the bottom rails and meeting at the stiffener (Fig. 14-3G). Check that the seat stands squarely on a level surface before finally fitting these struts.

10. If you want to make a single seat or chair, shorten the assembly to about 24 inches wide. There will be no need for a stiffener under the seat slats. Instead of the diagonal struts, put a single rail between the bottom end rails.

Materials List for Yard Seat

2 rear legs	3 x 3 x 37
2 front legs	3 x 3 x 24
2 bottom rails	1 x 3 x 21
2 seat rails	1 x 3 x 23
2 arm rests	1 x 3 x 22
7 slats	1 x 3 x 49
1 seat stiffener	1 x 3 x 14
2 diagonal struts	1 x 3 x 25

15

Jewelry Box

A POLISHED BOX MADE OF ATTRACTIVE HARD-wood to stand on a dresser is much more acceptable as a holder for jewelry than the plastic or metal boxes often used.

This box (Fig. 15-1) is intended to be made of wood of light sections, to have a reasonable capacity for jewelry (Fig. 15-2A). The same methods could be used for making a much larger box for other purposes. A tray with divisions is suggested. This lifts out, and the lid may be either lifted off or fitted with hinges.

Cutting wood to thin sections should be done with a fine saw and a fence set exactly square to it. Pieces cut in this way will require the minimum of planing and might only need sanding. All of the parts need not be the same wood. There could be a dark wood for the parts which show outside and a lighter color wood for the lining and tray.

There is a choice of box corner joints. They might be *dovetailed*, or you could cut *finger joints* (Fig. 15-2B), but a simple miter will not be strong enough. If one piece is cut into the other, pins both ways can supplement the glue (Fig. 15-2C). If you want to hide the end grain, a development of this joint includes a miter (Figs. 15-2D and 15-3A). The tray corners do not have to resist as much strain, and they may be simple laps with glue and pins, or you could repeat the corner joints chosen for the box corners.

The box and its lid are first made in one piece, then the table saw used to separate the two parts. Making it this way results in an exact match, which would be difficult if lid and box were made individually.

1. Prepare the wood for the box sides and ends, with the chosen joints marked out. If you are using finger joints, it is neat to arrange the fingers so the cut for the lid comes where two join (Fig. 15-2E), although this is not essential.

2. Join these parts, and from their overall sizes, mark out the top and bottom to overhang ⅜ inch all round (Figs. 15-2F and 15-3B). Round or mold the edges, but leave at least 1/16 inch flat outside the box edges.

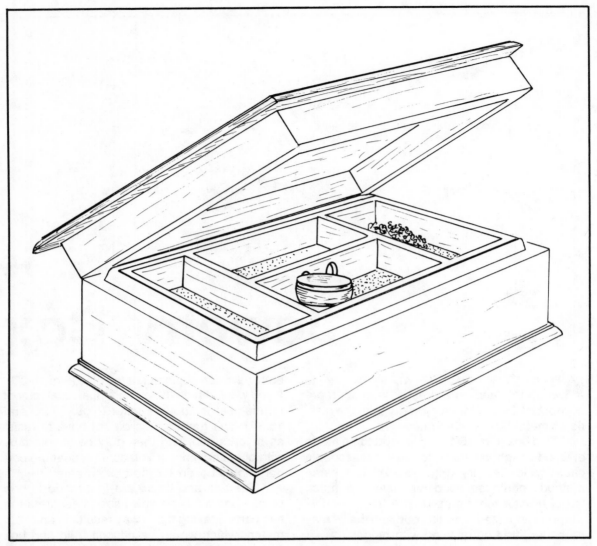

Fig. 15-1. This small box is intended for jewelry.

3. Glue the top and bottom on. Clamped glued joints should be adequate, but if you wish, a few pins may be driven and set below the surface to cover with wood filler. Pin heads under the bottom will not show, in any case.

4. Have the saw set only just high enough to cut all around to separate the lid from the box. Mark two adjoining edges, so the lid does not become reversed on the box, as it is unlikely that the box will be made with enough precision to

allow turning around without showing. Plane the cut edges.

5. Make the 3/16-inch lining to stand above the box edge about 3/8 inch all around (Figs. 15-2G and 15-3C). Bevel the outer surfaces slightly so the lid will fit easily. Miter the corners.

6. Put bearers 1/4-inch thick across the ends (Figs. 15-2H and 3D) to support the tray.

7. The tray parts are all 3/16-inch thick. The compartment arrangement shown (Fig. 15-3E)

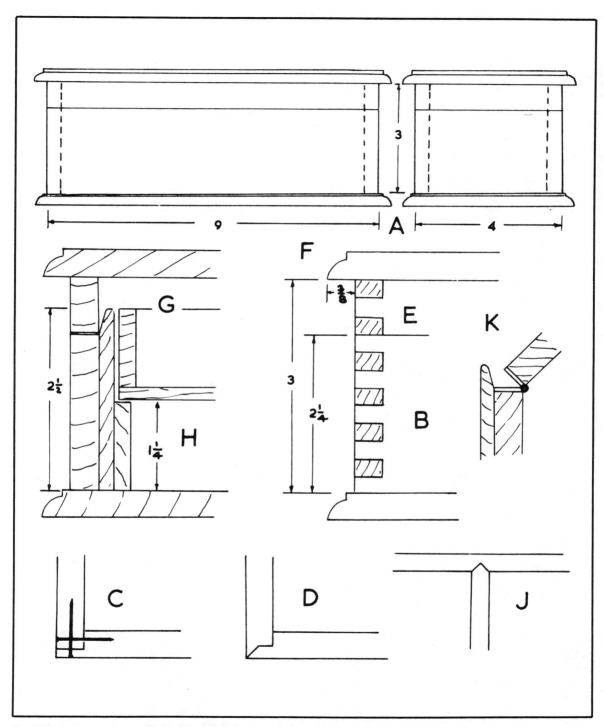

Fig. 15-2. Sizes, section, and alternative constructions for the jewelry box.

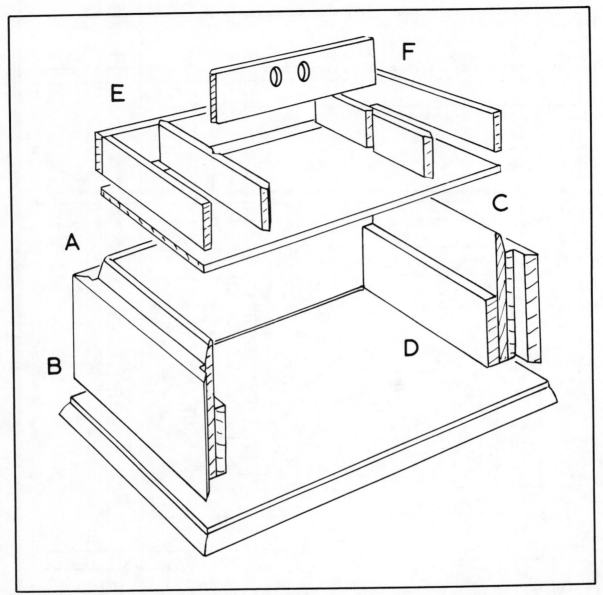

Fig. 15-3. How the parts of the jewelry box are arranged.

will probably suit your needs, but there may be variations. To lift the tray out, however, there has to be something to grip, such as two finger holes in the center part of this arrangement (Fig. 15-3F).

8. Mark out and cut the outside parts of the tray with the corners ready to be joined. In thin wood, a normal dado joint is inadvisable, and it is better to use triangular notches (Fig. 15-2J) for the divisions.

9. Assemble the tray with its bottom glued on. Make the size to drop easily into the box. Round the top and outside edges.

10. If the lid is to lift off, there is no other

constructional work to do. If the lid is to be hinged, choose hinges with flaps that match the thickness of the wood (Fig. 15-2K). They will probably be 1-inch long. A type with stops will prevent the lid falling too far back.

11. The box and tray bottoms may be lined with cloth, which may be glued in after complete assembly, but a way to get a neat fit is to arrange the cloth on the bottom before it is attached. Use nails or screws through the bottom to pull the joint tight, then trim off any cloth showing outside. To avoid marking the cloth, it would be advisable to do any inside staining or polishing before adding the cloth-covered bottom.

Materials List for Jewelry Box

2 sides	$3/8$	×	3	×	10
2 ends	$3/8$	×	3	×	5
1 top	$3/8$	×	$4\frac{3}{4}$	×	11
1 bottom	$3/8$	×	$4\frac{3}{4}$	×	11
2 liners	$3/16$	×	$2\frac{1}{2}$	×	9
2 liners	$3/16$	×	$2\frac{1}{2}$	×	4
2 supports	$1/4$	×	$1\frac{1}{4}$	×	4
2 tray sides	$1/4$	×	1	×	9
2 tray ends	$1/4$	×	1	×	4
1 tray bottom	$1/4$	×	3	×	9
3 tray divisions	$1/4$	×	1	×	4

16

Garden Gates and Fences

WITH ITS ABILITY TO CUT ANY NUMBER OF PIECES of wood to uniform width, a table saw is very suitable for making the parts for gates and several types of fences for use around the yard, garden, or other property. For many situations, the wood can be used direct from the saw. For more important positions, it may be planed before finishing with paint.

Although almost any wood might be used for a fence, certain of its characteristics should be considered. If it is not a durable wood, its life may be increased by treating with preservative. Most hardwoods can be expected to have a longer life than many softwoods, but that is not always so. A resinous straight-grained pine, with few knots, should last longer than some of the hardwoods, which are attractive as furniture, but do not stand up to exposure very well.

Besides durability, any tendency to warp or twist must be considered. If you start with unseasoned wood, it will shrink and twist, which may not matter for a field fence, but would be most unsatisfactory around the home yard. Even some seasoned wood may distort after it has become soaked with rain. If you want a fence board to keep its shape, avoid very twisted grain and frequent or large knots. If a knot in softwood has a black border, it will soon fall out. Would a hole in the fence matter?

Gates usually have to fit an opening and remain stable, without expanding or twisting, so choose seasoned wood without flaws, if later trouble is to be avoided.

Some durable woods weather to an attractive appearance without treatment, but most woods need protection. There are colored preservatives, which may suit your needs. Not all preservatives can be followed with paint—check with your supplier. Several coats of paint provide good protection, but be prepared to touch up periodically.

A *ledge and brace assembly* is a typical example of a yard gate or door. A tall gate is shown (Fig. 16-1A), but a lower gate with only two ledges could be made in the same way. The design shown has close boards, but a similar con-

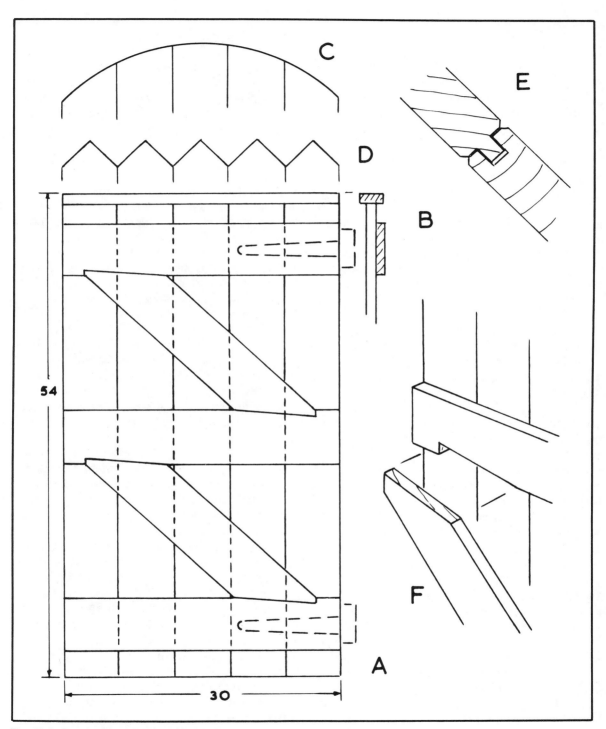

Fig. 16-1. Construction of a ledge and brace gate.

struction may be used with spaces between, if that would suit your needs. The top may be straight, preferably with a covering board (Fig. 16-1B). It might be curved (Fig. 16-1C), or cut with points (Fig. 16-1D) to match a fence or discourage attempts to climb over.

Board edges may be just cut square, or you could make tongue and groove joints (Fig. 16-1E), which prevent open gaps if the wood shrinks. Wood for this door may be $7/8$-inch-by-5-inches or 6 inches for all parts.

Any door will tend to sag if it is not properly braced. Even with braces it may be advisable to make the door a degree or so above square to the hinged side, to allow for settling. In this door, the two braces are notched into the ledges (Fig. 16-1F). Fit these joints closely to resist sag and always slope upwards from the hinged side.

A gate with a more solid appearance can be made with $1/2$-inch exterior plywood panels each side. The example (Fig. 16-2A) is shown as a low type (Fig. 16-2B), but the construction could be used for many other sizes. The internal parts may be softwood. All joints should be glued and pinned or screwed. With a painted finish, pin heads will not show. There need be no fitted joints between the internal parts—they merely butt closely together. The glued plywood will provide adequate strength.

Cut the two plywood panels slightly oversize, but mark the final outline on one of them. Use this as a guide for cutting the internal pieces, which may be $3/4$-inch thick, to give a total gate thickness of $1 3/4$ inches. Widths are about 2 inches at sides and bottom, with a strip wide enough to cut the curve at the top (Fig. 16-2C) and a stiffener across the middle (Fig. 16-2D), which is positioned to take screws from a latch or other fastener.

Join the inside pieces to one panel. Check that the surfaces are level and add the other plywood. When the glue has set, plane the edges level and square. Glue $1/4$-inch strips (Fig. 16-2E) to cover the plywood at the sides.

Unless you have chosen a very shallow curve for the top, you will probably not be able to bend a strip of single thickness over it. Instead

it will be easier and more satisfactory, as internal stress is removed, to use two thicknesses of about $3/16$-inch (Fig. 16-2F). Laminate in position, using wood too wide, plenty of glue, and enough pins to draw the wood tight. After the glue has set, trim the edges to a rounded overhang. At the ends of the top, make sure the door edges are covered to prevent water seeping into the inside.

Ordinary hinges, about 4 inches long, can be used between the gate and its post, and any type of fastener may be added. Protect the wood with plenty of paint.

There are several ways of building a wood fence. All depend on posts of either wood or concrete. The general arrangement of boards may be vertical or horizontal. For a special effect, you could set them diagonally. They may be arranged with spaces between or set close for maximum privacy or to form a wind break.

Wood posts should be 3 inches or more square, or 2 inches by 4 inches section. If the post is to be driven, point it on the saw, but do not go to a fine tip (Fig. 16-3A), which will crumble. Leave some extra length at the top, then trim to a point (Fig. 16-3B), a curve, or a slope (Fig. 16-3C) in position, so water will run off. Cut any joints before driving.

A simple fence may have boards nailed on horizontally (Fig. 16-3D). If you make the spacing the same as the boards and put more boards on the opposite side, the result is a fence that does not present a solid resistance to a breeze, but gives good privacy (Fig. 16-3E).

Close boarding may be nailed on in the same way and this is protected and looks good with a *capping* (Fig. 16-3F). Let boards butt together on a post (Fig. 16-3G) and overlap at corners (Fig. 16-3H). If you drive the nails in a dovetail fashion (Fig. 16-3J), it will be stronger than straight nailing.

For a picket fence with upright palings, there have to be horizontal rails. If you nail rails to posts, then nail upright pieces to them, the assembly stands forward. A neater way is to notch the rails into the posts and put a paling in front of a post of the same width (Fig. 16-4A).

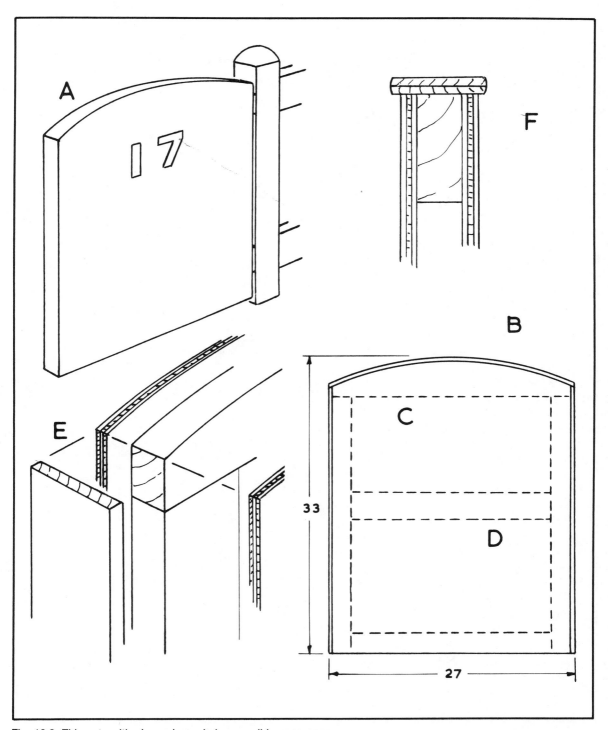

Fig. 16-2. This gate with plywood panels has a solid appearance.

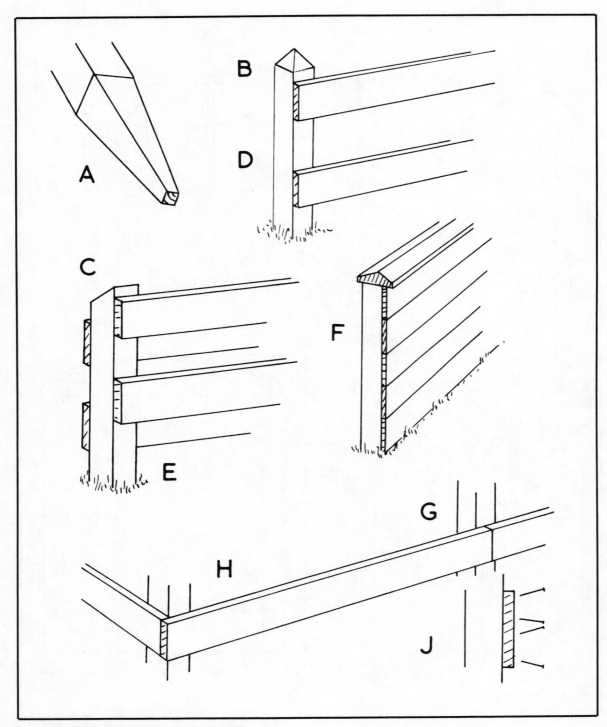

Fig. 16-3. Details of fences with horizontal rails.

74

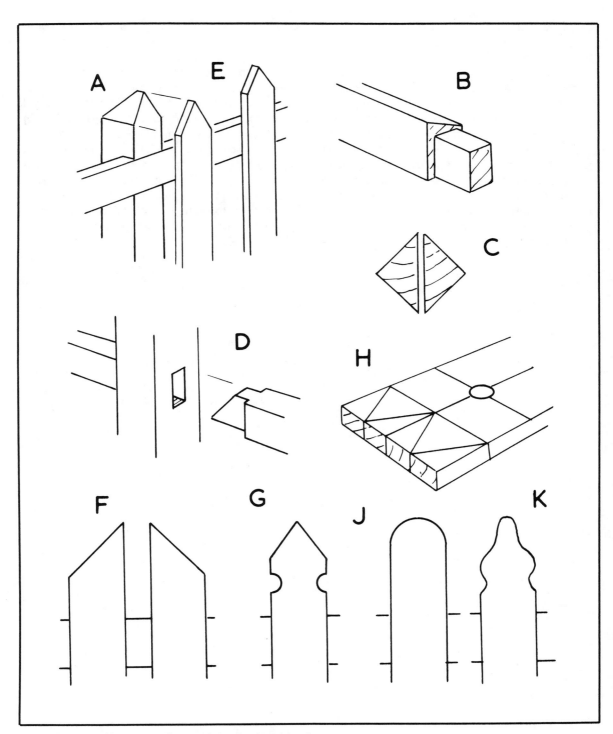

Fig. 16-4. Alternative constructions and details of a picket fence.

The more usual way is to join the rails into the posts so the paling and post fronts finish level. The joints may be mortise and tenon. So the rails do not trap water, which will encourage rot, bevel the top edges and cut down the tenon to suit (Fig. 16-4B). Such a rail may be 3 inches by 2 inches section. Another good way of being certain of shedding water is to cut a larger square section diagonally (Fig. 16-4C). Make tenons square to the face and as large as possible. Where tenons meet, they may be cut into each other (Fig. 16-4D). Although joints may be glued, using waterproof glue, you could just drive dowels through the tenons.

Upright boards may be close and have a capping similar to that suggested for horizontal close boarding. It is more usual to use this type of construction for open palings. Tops may be decorated as you wish, but there will be a large number of pieces to deal with, so choose decoration that can be cut easily to match and will not be too laborious. A point is usual (Fig. 16-4E). A slope is easier (Fig. 16-4F). A variation has curved hollows (Fig. 16-4G), made by drilling two boards together (Fig. 16-4H). Curved tops can be anything from semicircles (Fig. 16-4J) to shaped points (Fig. 16-4K). Post tops may have top shapes to complement the palings, and a gate could be made to match.

17

Paneled Cabinet

FRAMED PLYWOOD ALLOWS ATTRACTIVE FURNI-
ture to be made economically and without using very much solid wood. Grooves must be
made for the plywood with a table saw or by
other means. If you have facilities for doing that,
construction is straightforward. The framed
panels may be joined with dowels for a strong
assembly.

This *cabinet* (Fig. 17-1) is made by assem-
bling several framed plywood panels, then joining them with dowels. The top, shelf, and bottom
are solid wood or thicker plywood with solid
wood edging. All of the framing is 1-inch-
by-2-inch section, and the plywood panels are
⅜-inch thick.

The sizes (Fig. 17-2A) are for a cabinet at
table height and of a suitable size for use in the
home or shop, but variations would not affect the
method of building. A furniture-quality hardwood
and veneered plywood would make a cabinet to
match other furniture. Softwood may be used for
a painted finish. A cabinet with a strong solid top
can form the base for a machine in your shop.

1. The back, front, and side panels all
have similar legs (Fig. 17-2B), except that the
front legs do not need grooves. Make the
grooves to suit your plywood and ½ inch deep
(Fig. 17-2C). Cut the shaped feet on the legs.

2. Make the rails to fit between the legs,
with tenons to fit tightly in the grooves (Fig.
17-2D). Start with the pair of side framed panels
(Fig. 17-3A). Cut the plywood to size and assemble the sides to match each other.

3. Cut the rails for the back. Make a similar one without a groove for the front. Front and
back fit between the sides (Figs. 17-2E and
17-3B). Assemble the back. Cut mortises for the
rail in the tops of the front legs. Mark and drill
for ⅜-inch dowels, at about 6-inch intervals,
where the legs will meet.

4. If there is to be a shelf, put bearers on
each side, cut back to clear the front and back
legs (Fig. 17-3C). Make the bearers this length,
even if the shelf is to be narrower.

5. Prepare the bottom (Fig. 17-3D) to fit
between the bottom rails of the sides and back

Fig. 17-1. This floor-standing cabinet makes use of framed plywood panels.

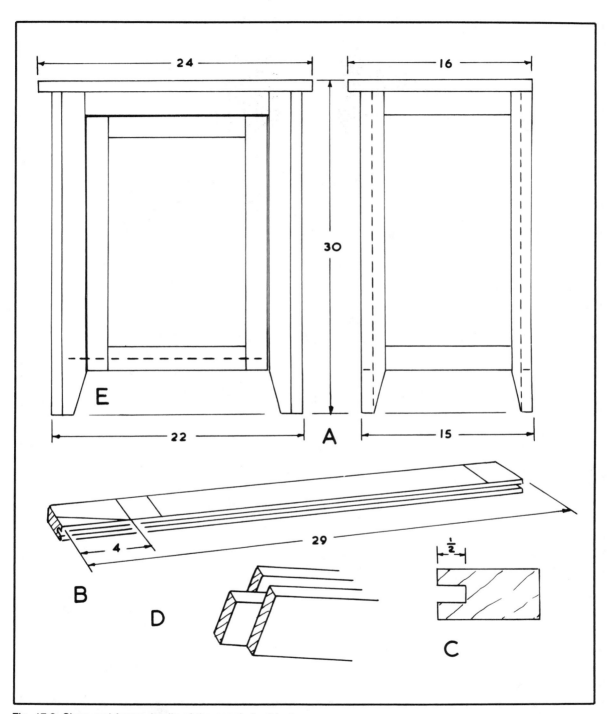

Fig. 17-2. Sizes and frame details of the paneled cabinet.

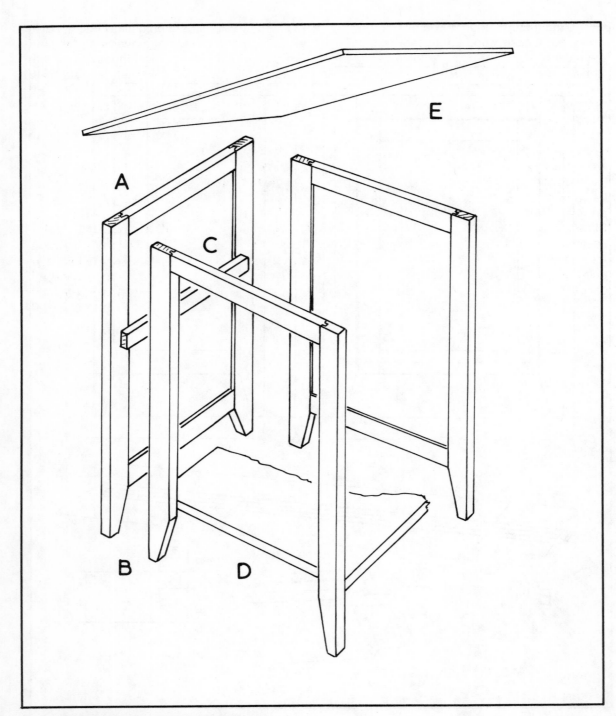

Fig. 17-3. The main parts of the paneled cabinet.

and inside the front legs. If you use ¾-inch plywood, put a solid wood lip across the front for the sake of appearance in better quality work. Drill for dowels into the rails and the front legs.

6. Glue and dowel the parts together. The bottom should hold the parts square, but see that the assembly stands level.

7. The shelf may just rest in place, if you want it removable, or it may be screwed to its bearers to provide additional stiffening.

8. Make the top (Fig. 17-3E) level with the back, if the cabinet is to come close to a wall, and overhanging about 1 inch on front and sides. Plywood may be lipped with solid wood. For a solid top, glue together sufficient boards. Edges may be molded, if you wish. Fit the top with glue and dowels. One dowel in each leg top and one or two intermediately on each rail are enough.

9. Make the door in a similar way to the main panels. Its size should allow it to fit easily between the front legs and overhang the cabinet bottom. Use two 2-inch hinges at one side and fit a handle and fastener at the other side.

Materials List for Paneled Cabinet

8 legs	1	×	2	× 30
4 rails	1	×	2	× 15
3 rails	1	×	2	× 22
2 shelf bearers	1	×	2	× 15
1 top	1	× 16	× 25	
2 door sides	1	×	2	× 24
2 door rails	1	×	2	× 14
2 panels	13	× 24	× ⅜ plywood	
1 panel	18	× 24	× ⅜ plywood	
1 panel	14	× 22	× ⅜ plywood	
1 shelf	10	× 22	× ¾ plywood	
1 bottom	13	× 22	× ¾ plywood	

18

Plant Stands

IF YOU HAVE A FLOWERING PLANT IN A POT, PARTIC-
ularly if it is a type that spreads and hangs
downwards, it is best displayed on a high stand,
preferably alone, where its individual beauty can
be appreciated. Suitable stands are made like
high tables. The two examples shown (Fig. 18-1)
will support a plant pot at the same height, but
one has four legs and the other has three. Three
legs are particularly appropriate where the
ground is uneven. Four legs might wobble, but
three will stand firm.

Because the feet need to be spread for sta-
bility, both stands make use of angle cuts on the
table saw; the three-legged one being particularly interesting. Both stands could have
round tops, but a square top is appropriate to
four legs and a hexagonal top suits three legs.

Tops may be solid wood, plywood, or
veneered particleboard. They should be water-
resistant, because there is always a risk of get-
ting damp from the plant. The legs should be
fairly straight-grained, so any later risk of twisting or warping is reduced. Hardwood may be

polished, but painted softwood is satisfactory.

The square stand has crossing rails under
the top and lighter crossing rails 12 inches from
the floor (Fig. 18-2A).

1. To get the angles to cut and the lengths
of parts, set out the main lines.

2. Make the four legs slightly too long.
Keep them parallel, 4 inches wide for 6 inches
at the top, then taper to 3 inches.

3. Make the crossing top rails to the angles obtained from your drawing and with a halving joint at the center (Fig. 18-2B). The tenons
are 2 inches deep and long enough to go
through the legs and project enough for rounded
ends.

4. Cut matching mortises in the legs and
bevel the tops to suit (Fig. 18-2C). Cut the legs
to length and bevel their feet parallel with the
floor.

5. From your setting out, get the positions
of the bottom rails on the legs and mark them.
Make the crossing bottom rails. Tenons on the

Fig. 18-1. Two plant stands: with three legs and four legs.

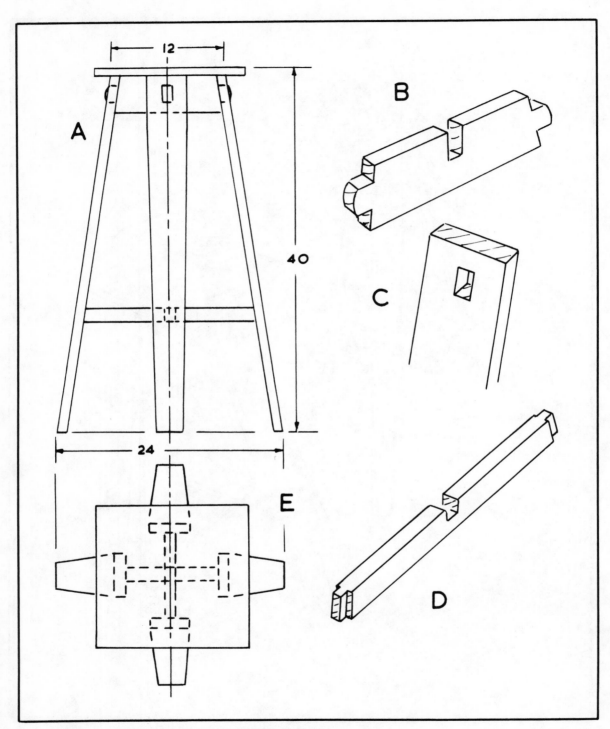

Fig. 18-2. Sizes and construction of the four-legged plant stand.

84

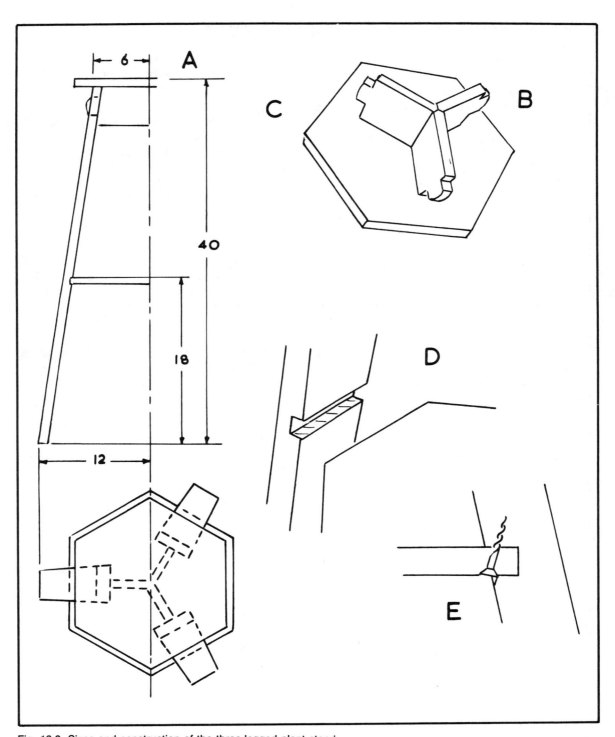

Fig. 18-3. Sizes and construction of the three-legged plant stand.

ends need not go right through. They may stop at half thickness (Fig. 18-2D).

6. The top is a 16-inch square (Fig. 18-2E). Corners may be rounded or beveled.

7. Assemble both sets of rails squarely. Add the legs and see that the assembly stands square and without twist.

8. Glue on the top with a ⅜-inch dowel near the end of each rail.

9. The three-legged stand is similar in several ways to the square stand, but because of the triangular arrangement, there can't be rails crossing with halved joints (Fig. 18-3).

10. Set out the main lines of half a side view (Fig. 18-3A).

11. The top rails are in three parts, meeting at the center (Fig. 18-3B). From your setting out, mark one of these pieces, with tenons similar to those on the square stand. From this, mark out and cut three of them, angled to meet at the center.

12. Make the top (Fig. 18-3C) 16 inches across the flats of the hexagon. On the underside of this mark the positions of the rails. Drill for two dowels in each rail, then assemble the rails to the top.

13. Make the legs similar in overall shape to those of the square stand.

14. Make a hexagonal shelf to the size obtained from your setting out and notch the legs to take it (Fig. 18-3D).

15. Glue the legs to the top rails and glue the shelf into its notches. For extra security drive a thin screw upwards under the center of each shelf joint (Fig. 18-3E).

Materials List for Plant Stands

Four-Legged Stand

4 legs	1	×	4	×	42
2 top rails	1	×	4	×	16
2 bottom rails	1	×	1½	×	21
1 top	¾	×	16	×	16

Three-Legged Stand

3 legs	1	×	4	×	42
3 top rails	1	×	4	×	8
1 shelf	½	×	18	×	18
1 top	¾	×	16	×	19

19

Matching Table
and Benches

A TABLE LARGE ENOUGH FOR A MEAL FOR SEV-eral people has to be made of fairly stout wood, but if your table saw is able to cut hardwood up to 1¾ inches thick, most of the cuts can be done on it if your wood is obtained already machined to thickness. This table (Fig. 19-1) could be made alone, but it is shown with matching benches, made in the same way, although of lighter section wood. If made of a good quality hardwood and finished by polishing, these items are suitable for use indoors. A similar set, made of a durable wood or treated with preservative, could be used on a deck or patio and left outside for most of the year.

Assembly is described with mortise and tenon joints for the main parts, for a traditional construction, but dowels may be used. Tenons can be cut accurately on the table saw and mortises shaped mostly with a drill. Solid wood is used for all parts, but the top could be made of framed plywood, for economical production.

This type of *refectory table* is made with end pedestals, which are built as units; then they are

joined with one or more rails and the top added last. The benches are made in the same way to a reduced size.

As shown (Fig. 19-2A), the table has a top 27 inches wide and a length of 54 inches. If the benches are made with tops 12 inches wide and a length that fits easily between the table pedestals, they will push under the table until stopped by the lengthwise rail and will then be completely under the table and out of the way (Fig. 19-2B). The table top is 29 inches high and the seat tops 16 inches high. These are common heights, but you may want to check the heights of existing tables and seats, if you wish them to match. If you alter heights very much, make sure the vertical rail between the table pedestals is in a suitable position to act as a stop when the benches are pushed in.

1. Prepare the wood for the table pedestals. All parts are 1¾ inches thick. Top and bottom have the same outlines, but rails tenon into the top, and there are blocks forming feet

87

Fig. 19-1. A table with matching and stowing benches.

under the bottoms.

2. Mark out the tops (Fig. 19-2C). Allow for the uprights tenoning into the edge and mortises for the top rails ½ inch outside the upright position, then taper to half thickness at the ends.

3. Mark out the bottoms in the same way, but without the mortises for the rails. Feet 1-inch

thick and 4 inches long will go under the ends.

4. Mark out the uprights (Fig. 19-2D) with tenons 1-inch long to match the mortises. Mark the position of the main lengthwise rail and the mortises (Fig. 19-2E).

5. Make the two top rails, with tenons cut across to suit the direction of the grain of the

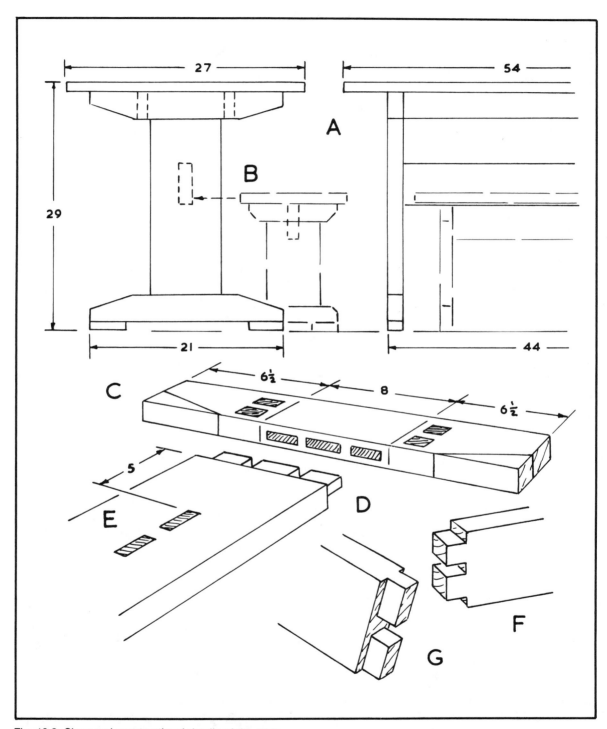

Fig. 19-2. Sizes and constructional details of the table.

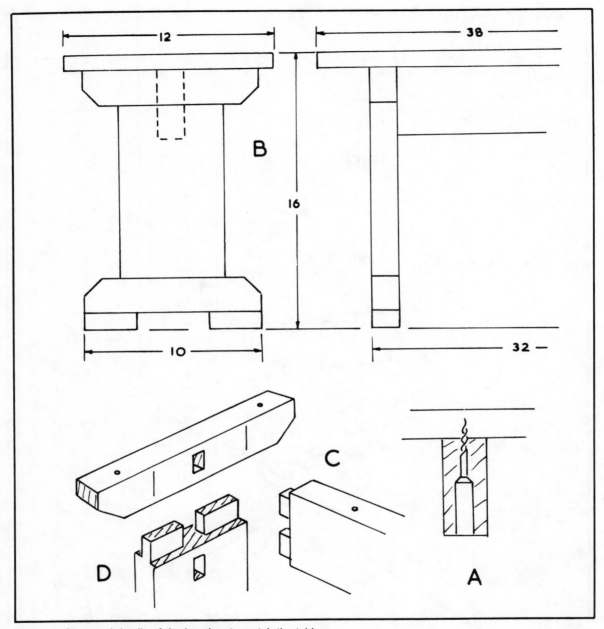

Fig. 19-3. Sizes and details of the benches to match the table.

pedestal tops (Fig. 19-2F).

6. Make the main lengthwise rail with tenons to suit the vertical grain of the upright part of the pedestal (Fig. 19-2G). Tenons in all rails could be 1-inch long.

7. Cut the mortises to match the tenons and finish shaping the pedestal parts. Glue them together, including the feet. See that they match.

8. Prepare the top rails for counterbored screws upwards into the top (Fig. 19-3A), at

about 12-inch intervals. Drill near the ends of the pedestal tops similarly. After assembly, you may glue plugs in the holes, but as they are underneath, they may not matter.

9. Join the pedestals with the rails. Check that the pedestals are upright and the assembly is square by comparing diagonals. Stand it on a level surface while the glue sets.

10. Make the top by gluing sufficient boards to make up the width. A traditional refectory table top has square edges, but you could round or mold them, if you wish.

11. Invert the framework on the underside of the top and locate it centrally. Screw through the holes, but do not use glue. The top may then expand and contract slightly without the risk of cracking.

12. The benches have a generally similar appearance to the table, but there is only a single rail between the pedestals (Fig. 19-3B).

13. Make the two pairs of pedestals in the same way as for the table, except there must be an allowance for the mortise and tenon joints both ways under the top.

14. Mark out a rail so there is one tenon into the top of the pedestal and one into the upright (Fig. 19-3C). Arrange the tenons from the uprights into the top of a pedestal far enough

apart to clear the mortises the other way (Fig. 19-3D).

15. Drill for screws upwards into the rails and ends in the same way as for the table top. Assemble the bench frameworks, checking squareness and freedom from twist.

16. When you cut the boards for the tops, make the length an easy fit inside the table pedestals. A clearance of 1-inch at each end will allow the benches to be pushed in without trouble.

17. Lightly round all exposed edges of the table and benches before applying a finish. Make sure there is no sharpness on the bench feet so floor covering will not be damaged.

Materials List for Matching Table and Benches

4 table pedestals	1¾	×	3	×	23
2 table pedestals	1¾	×	8	×	25
4 table feet	1	×	1¾	×	5
2 table top rails	1	×	3	×	45
1 table rail	1½	×	5	×	45
1 table top	1¼	×	27	×	56
8 bench pedestals	1½	×	2	×	12
4 bench pedestals	1½	×	6	×	13
8 bench feet	1	×	1½	×	4
2 bench rails	1½	×	4	×	32
2 bench tops	1¼	×	12	×	40

20

Bed Ends

A BED MAY BE USED WITHOUT A HEAD OR FOOT, but something at the head improves appearance and adds to comfort by providing a place to lean against or prevent pillows falling off, as well as making the unit into a whole. There is not such a good case for a foot board, although it was not so long ago that all beds had matching foot and head boards. If you want to make a bed in the traditional way, the foot can be made like the head, but with less projection; although if you prefer no visible foot board you can settle for a lower mattress support.

Modern mattresses or their supports are arranged to either attach directly to the legs or rest on iron assemblies which do. Older bed assemblies had wood sides to support the mattress and these were attached to the legs in several ways, all of which could be disassembled so the bed could be reduced to pieces portable through doors and stairs. For the purpose of this project, it is assumed that the bed sides can be attached with metal or other fittings to the legs and

no special work has to be done to the legs to accommodate them.

The width of a bed must suit the width of the mattress supports. Before making the bed ends have the mattress ready, so its width can be measured. There are many widths, but in these examples, a width of 54 inches across the outside of the legs is used, and you must modify this to suit your mattress.

Legs are usually on casters and about 2 inches should be allowed for them when settling on heights. There can be considerable rocking strain on legs and they must be stiff enough—2-inch square straight-grained hardwood is advisable. Other parts will normally be hardwood, unless you want to feature knotty pine or other softwood.

SIMPLE BED ENDS

A typical simple pair of bed ends (Fig. 20-1A) has solid boards notched into the legs, and this provides a general guide to sizes (Fig. 20-1B) that

92

may be applied to other arrangements. The head has a rail for stiffness at about the level of the bed sides (Fig. 20-1C). If you want to make the bed ends without a foot board, stop the legs at mattress level and include a stiffening lower rail (Fig. 20-1D).

A suitable curve for the boards may be drawn along a lath bent around nails (Fig. 20-1E), or you can improvise a compass with a long lath and an awl (Fig. 20-1F).

Notch the legs to about half the board thickness. Avoid spoiling the front appearance by using counterbored and plugged screws from the back (Fig. 20-1G). Alternatively, use dowels in similar positions.

The lower rail at the head and parts of a lower foot are best tenoned (Fig. 20-1H) although they could be doweled.

Materials List for Simple Bed Ends

2 legs	2	×	2 × 41
2 legs	2	×	2 × 26
2 boards	1	×	18 × 55
1 rail	1¼	×	4 × 54

RAILED BED ENDS

An alternative to notching in a wide board is to make a bed end with several rails, tenoned or doweled into the legs, so the appearance is something like a fence. Arrange the rails fairly closely, particularly if children are involved, so a small head cannot be pushed through.

This bed head (Fig. 20-2A) has four rails, with the top one curved. The foot may be made with two or three rails. If you do not want a visible foot board, you can follow sizes and proportions suggested for the previous example.

Mark out the posts (Fig. 20-2B), including mortise and tenon joints or dowels. Mark and cut the rails to suit. The posts should extend at least 1 inch above the top rail joint. If you have the use of a lathe, turned finials (Fig. 20-2C) would look good. You could shape to a cone (Fig. 20-2D) or round the tops (Fig. 20-2E).

Shape the top rail. It may also be decorated

with a pattern of holes (Fig. 20-2F) or a piercing. Round the edges of all rails in cross-section, so there is nothing sharp exposed.

Materials List for Railed Bed Ends

2 posts	2 × 2 × 40
4 rails	1 × 4 × 54
1 rail	1 × 6 × 54

PANELED BED END

Instead of solid wood, a head board may be made by framing plywood panels. It is possible to include the legs in the framing, so the rails join into the legs and the plywood fits into grooves in the legs as well as the frames. An alternative, which is described here, is to make up a framed panel and fit it into notched legs in a similar way to the first example (Fig. 20-3A). A foot panel may be the same as the head panel, but at a lower level. A simple symmetrical arrangement of rails and panels is shown, but you could arrange intermediate parts sloping or curved, divisions across as well as vertically, gaps between panels, or you can express your own ideas by originating your own pattern, but remember that the main purpose of the bed end is to keep bedding in place.

Legs and lower rails are the same as in the first example. The paneled frame is made as a unit to fit with counterbored screws in the same way as the solid board.

The parts of the frame are all 1-inch-by-2-inch section, except a piece 4 inches wide is needed if you want to shape the top. Plywood panels may be ¼-inch or ⅜-inch thick, preferably veneered to match the surrounding wood. Groove the framing ½ inch deep to suit the plywood (Fig. 20-3B). Groove the intermediate strips on both sides (Fig. 20-3C). Cut tenons on the upright parts to fit tightly in the grooves (Fig. 20-3D).

Make the horizontal rails too long at first, so they can be trimmed after assembly. Mark on the positions of the upright parts (Fig. 20-3E). To get the top shape symmetrical make a *tem-*

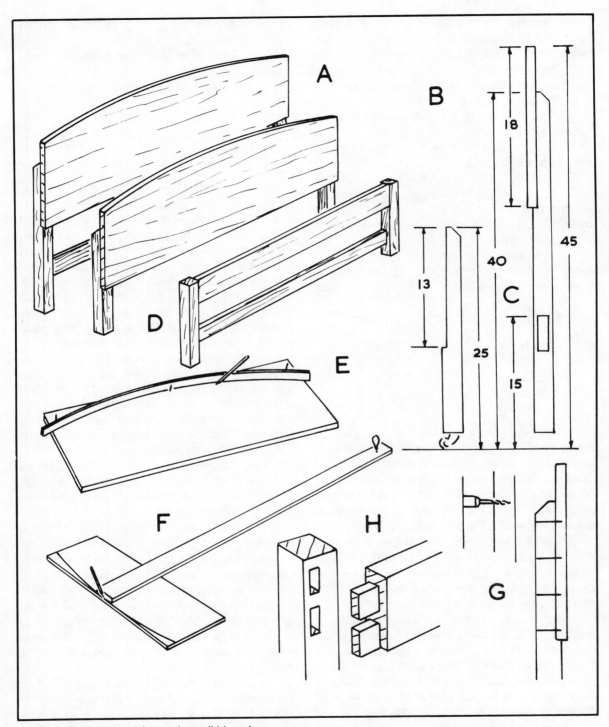

Fig. 20-1. Bed head and foot, using solid boards.

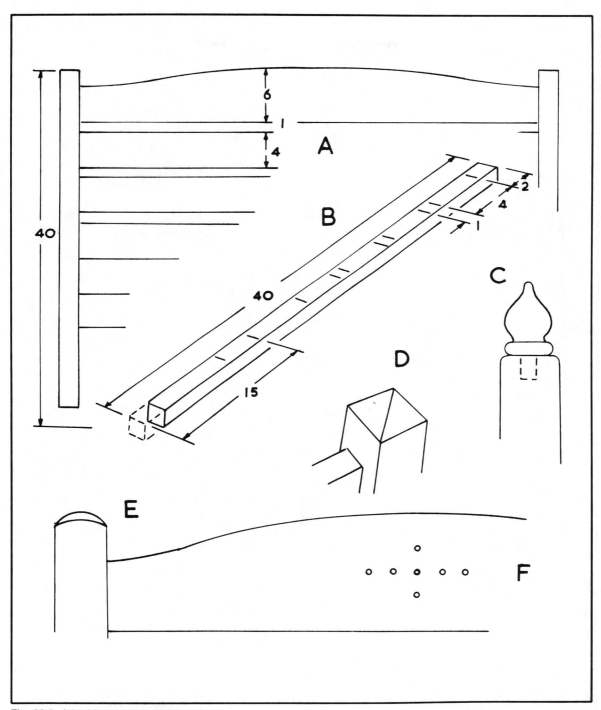

Fig. 20-2. A bed head with horizontal rails.

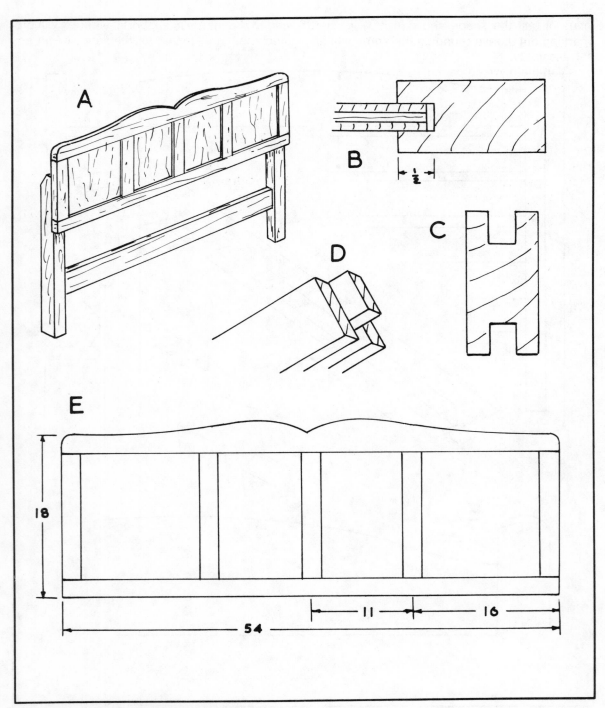

Fig. 20-3. A bed head with framed plywood panels.

plate of half the shape and turn it over when marking out. Leave rounding the ends until after assembly.

Cut the plywood panels to size, so they do not touch the bottoms of their grooves and the tenon shoulders can be clamped tight. Glue these parts, then trim the ends level. Round all exposed edges. Make the legs and lower rail in the same way as for the first example, then fit the framed assembly with glue and counterbored screws.

If you make a foot board, the panel may be the same and located low enough to cover the end of the mattress supports, where it will provide enough stiffening for the legs without any rails across.

Materials List for Paneled Bed End

2 legs	2	×	2 × 41	
1 rail	1¼	×	4 × 54	
1 panel frame	1	×	2 × 55	
1 panel frame	1	×	4 × 55	
5 panel frames	1	×	2 × 17	
2 panels	15	×	15 × ⅜ plywood	
2 panels	11	×	15 × ⅜ plywood	

21

Desk

A FLAT-TOPPED TABLE WITH STORAGE SPACE BE-
low will form a desk for home or office. It may
also serve as a hobby work table with space underneath for all the hobby equipment. When out
of use, it will not look out of place in a living room
and may even serve as an extra table for meals.

Such a desk may be made of solid wood
and plywood, but this design (Fig. 21-1) is particularly suitable for veneered particleboard, and
all parts of this desk are intended to be made
of particleboard about ¾-inch thick, bought already veneered on both sides and with matching strip veneer to cover cut edges. The veneer
may be plastic or wood. The resin in particleboard quickly blunts ordinary steel, so you
will get best results with a *carbide-tipped* saw
blade.

Most parts can be joined with ¼-inch
dowels at about 4-inch spacing. In some places,
you could use counterbored screws covered by
matching plastic plugs. Use glue as well where
possible.

The desk is formed of three units. The top

is a piece of particleboard. One support includes
shelves, which may serve as a bookcase. The
other support is a pedestal with a wide shelf and
an enclosed part with a door below that.

Use the general drawing (Fig. 21-2) as a
guide to sizes. The top overhangs the other parts
2 inches all around (Fig. 21-2A), so both supports
are 20 inches back to front and must be the
same height (Fig. 21-2B). If the parts are care-
fully and slowly sawn, the edges may be good
enough without planing, but plane and sand any
unevenness, so edge veneer will bond tightly.

1. Start with the block of shelves (Fig.
21-3). The sides are the full depth and the other
pieces fit between them. Cut the pieces to size
and veneer any outward edges.

2. Mark the positions of other parts on the
pairs of sides (Fig. 21-3A).

3. Glue and dowel the *plinth* under the
bottom shelf (Fig. 21-3B).

4. Mark and drill for dowels—three in
each shelf end and others at about 4-inch spac-

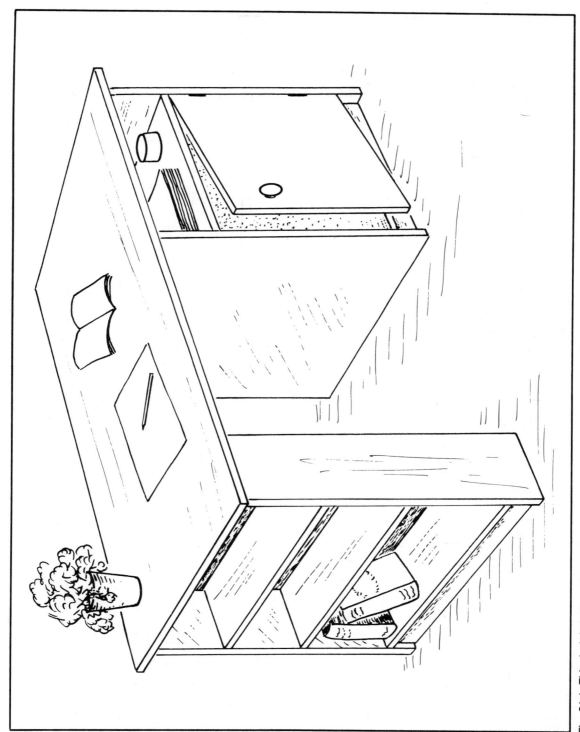

Fig. 21-1. This desk is built as three units.

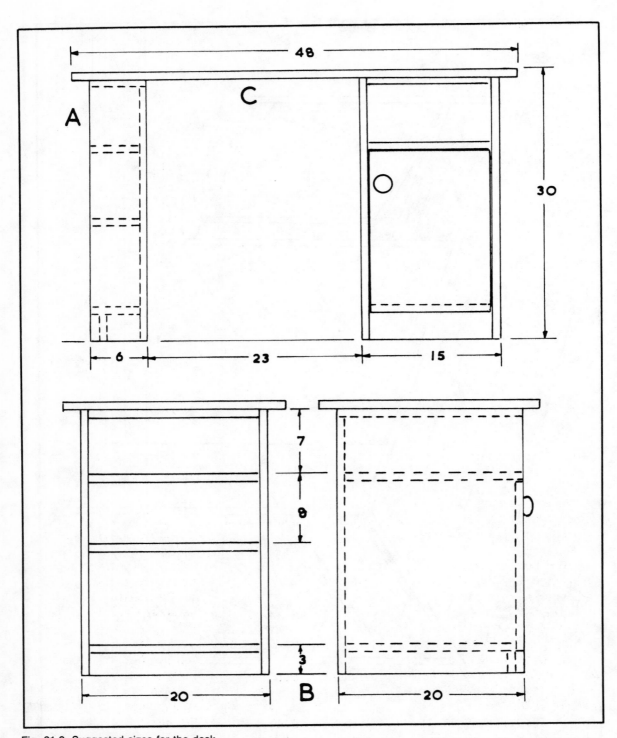

Fig. 21-2. Suggested sizes for the desk.

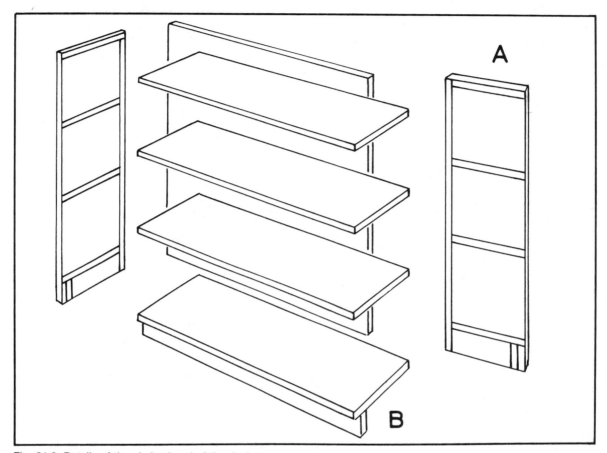

Fig. 21-3. Details of the shelved end of the desk.

ing in the back edges. Two dowels from the back into each shelf will strengthen the assembly.

5. Have glue and dowels ready. Assemble and clamp the unit.

6. The other pedestal is marked out in a similar way, with the positions of its crosswise parts marked first on the pair of sides (Fig. 21-4A).

7. The back fits between the sides, and the top two shelves are full width (Fig. 21-4B).

8. Cut the bottom shelf back so the door will close over it (Fig. 21-4C). Fit the plinth under it, either level with the front edge or set back a little (Fig. 21-4D).

9. Cut the pieces to size and veneer any outward edges.

10. Glue and dowel the plinth under the bottom shelf.

11. Mark and drill for dowels in all other joints, then assemble this unit.

12. Make the door to fit between the sides, under the middle shelf, and to overhang the bottom shelf. Fit hinges to one side and a handle and fastener to the other side (Fig. 21-4E).

13. Square the board for the top and veneer its edges (Fig. 21-2C).

14. With the top inverted, mark on it the positions of the supports.

15. Drill and screw upwards. Arrange a screw near the corner of each part and as many other screws as are needed to provide strong joints.

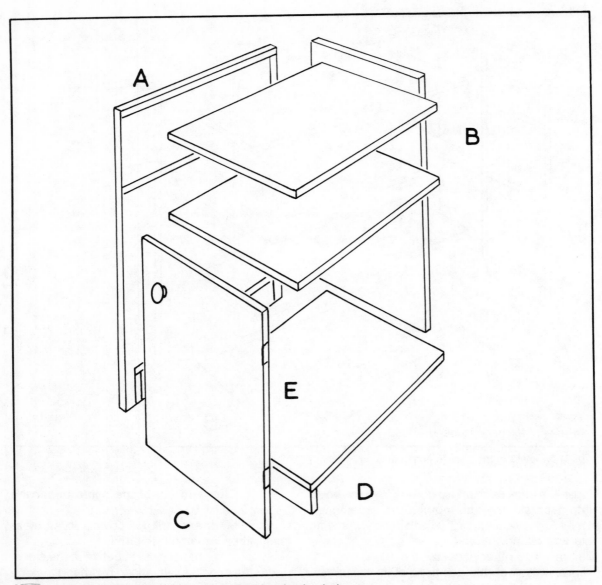

Fig. 21-4. Details of the parts of the main pedestal under the desk.

Materials List for Desk
(All ¾-inch veneered particleboard)

1 top	24	×	48	2 sides	20	× 30
2 sides	6	×	30	2 shelves	13½	× 20
4 shelves	5¼	×	20	1 shelf	13½	× 19¼
1 plinth	2¼	×	20	1 plinth	2¼	× 19
1 back	18½	×	30	1 door	18½	× 20

22

Bar or Counter

A WORKING SURFACE HIGHER THAN A TABLE IS useful when standing or sitting on a high stool. It also acts as a divider or serving place when people have to be kept away from stored drinks or food. Usually, there has to be an attractive appearance at the front, while the back is arranged to permit storage of many things, and appearance there is less important than utility. This bar or counter (Fig. 22-1) is designed for such a purpose. If the back will be in view, as when the counter is used as a kitchen divider, there may be some strips covering edges or a curtain could be arranged across.

The structure is made up of frames, joined by nailing or screwing. Shelves are particleboard or plywood. The top is best made of particleboard, or other material, surfaced with something resistant to heat and most liquids. One end will probably come against a wall. The other end and front are covered first with hardboard, then with vertical strips, which slope back at the front and have a kicker strip below.

All the internal structure is softwood. Parts visible at the front and end should be hardwood. The decorative vertical strips might be all one attractive hardwood, or you could alternate light and dark woods. Most parts are made from two sections of wood so you can set up your saw and planer to prepare all you need in advance, then construction can be quite fast.

The sizes shown (Fig. 22-2A) will serve as a guide, to be modified to suit your needs. If you extend the bar much, have vertical frames at not more than 18-inch intervals.

1. The key parts are the four vertical frames, which are all the same (Fig. 22-3A) and made with 1-inch-by-2-inch wood halved at all crossings. Have the parts square to the back, but taper the front. Corner halving joints (Fig. 22-3B) may be cut on the saw, but the intermediate waste will have to be chiseled. Join with glue and nails or screws.

2. The top and bottom frames (Fig. 22-3C) fit above and below the vertical frames. Check their widths against the tops and bottoms of

Fig. 22-1. This bar or counter fits against a wall.

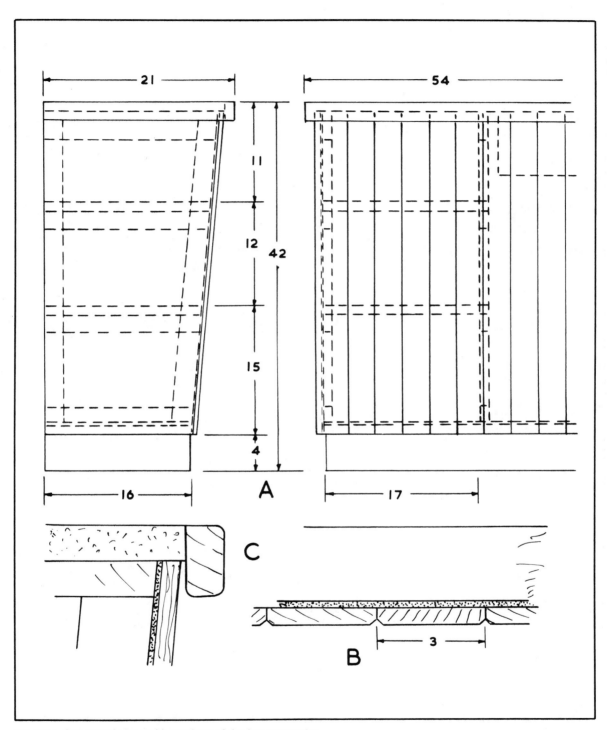

Fig. 22-2. Suggested sizes with sections of the bar or counter.

105

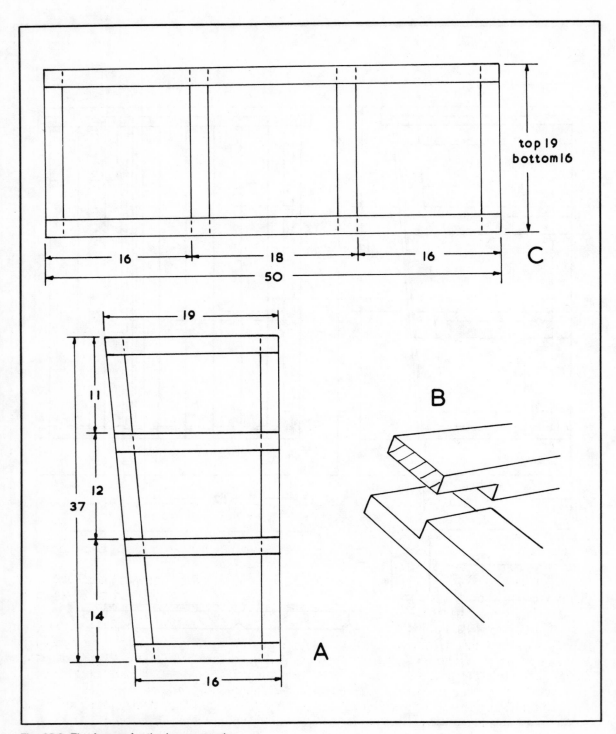

Fig. 22-3. The frames for the bar or counter.

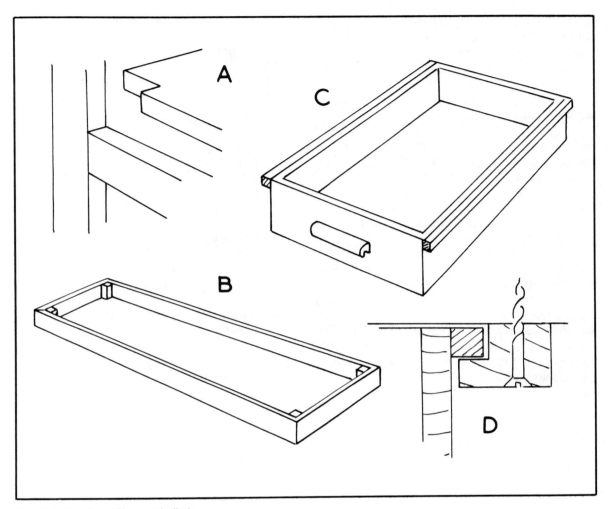

Fig. 22-4. The bar drawer and plinth.

these frames and bevel the front edges to match them. Use halving joints at all crossings.

3. Cover the bottom frame with plywood, glued and nailed on.

4. Cover the end frame with hardboard.

5. Assemble the frames by screwing or nailing. See that the assembly is square. If necessary, put a temporary diagonal brace across until other parts hold the counter true.

6. Make shelves to fit into the vertical frames. They could be thick plywood, but plastic-surfaced particleboard will be easier to clean. Notch around the uprights (Fig. 22-4A). Bevel the

edges to match the front slope. Glue and screw in place.

7. Cover the front with hardboard, using glue and pins to the shelf edges as well as the frames.

8. To cover the front and end, prepare strips. These are shown ½-inch-by-3-inches (Fig. 22-2B), but they may be any reasonable section to suit your stock. A light bevel on front edges will improve appearance.

9. Fit the strips closely with pins through the hardboard into the framing.

10. For the kickboard or *plinth,* make a

boxed frame that will come level at the back and set back a little at the covered edges. It will look best with mitered corners, which may be strengthened with blocks glued inside (Fig. 22-4B).

11. Fit this assembly with screws downwards through the bottom frame.

12. Make the top to come level at the back and against the wall, but projecting slightly over the covered parts (Fig. 22-2C). Cover the edge with a strip, mitered at the front corner and well rounded where it may be handled. Screw upwards through the frame into the top.

13. One or more drawers may be required, and the simplest way to make them is to treat them as boxes slung below the top. Make a box with finger joints and plywood bottom. Fit divisions if you wish.

14. For hanging, put square strips along the top edges (Fig. 22-4C). Make two slides into which the drawer will fit (Fig. 22-4D) and screw them upwards into the top frame. The drawer may have its front hollowed to provide a grip, or you could add a handle.

Materials List for Bar or Counter.

8 uprights	1	×	2	×	40	
20 rails	1	×	2	×	20	
4 rails	1	×	2	×	52	
4 rails	1	×	2	×	17	
1 bottom	16	×	52	×	½	plywood
2 kickboards	1	×	4	×	50	
2 kickboards	1	×	4	×	17	
24 trims	½	×	3	×	40	
1 top	1	×	20	×	54	
1 top edge	1	×	2	×	55	
1 top edge	1	×	2	×	22	
4 shelves	¾	×	19	×	19	
1 front	39	×	54	×	⅛	hardboard
1 end	21	×	39	×	⅛	hardboard
2 drawer sides	½	×	5	×	19	
2 drawer ends	½	×	5	×	16	
1 drawer bottom	16	×	19	×	¼	plywood
2 drawer runners	½	×	½	×	19	
2 drawer slides	1	×	1½	×	19	

23

Toolbox

THE OLDTIME WOODWORKING CRAFTSMAN KEPT all his tools in a large box, which was so heavy without tools that it took two men to lift it, and when loaded with tools it needed a cart to take it to the next job. We have no use for such a box today, but a similar lighter and smaller box still has many applications. Besides its use in the shop for storing tools (possibly those less frequently required), it can also be used to transport sporting equipment, camping requirements, and activity gear. If it is made watertight and weatherproof, it will protect its contents during outdoor activities and can always be used as a seat.

This box (Fig. 23-1) is made of plywood framed externally, so the inside is smooth. With waterproof plywood and durable hardwood, and all parts joined with corrosion-resistant screws or nails, the finished box should stand up to almost any conditions and keep the contents unharmed. Strips 1-inch square and ½-inch exterior or marine plywood are used for most parts of the box (Fig. 23-2A). At the sizes shown, one person can reach to both handles and carry the box with a light load, while a second person can share if you pack in too much. Sizes may be varied without altering the method of construction.

1. Start with the two ends (Fig. 23-3A). Glue and nail strips to the outer surfaces and plane the plywood level.

2. Cut plywood for the sides to match the depth of the ends. Put strips along top and bottom edges (Fig. 23-3B).

3. Glue and screw the sides to the ends. Where the outer strips overlap, glue ½-inch dowels in the joints (Fig. 23-2B).

4. Level the bottom edges, if necessary, and attach the bottom plywood (Fig. 23-3C). Put strips across underneath the ends to act as feet (Fig. 23-3D).

5. There could be metal or rope handles attached to the ends, but simple handles are

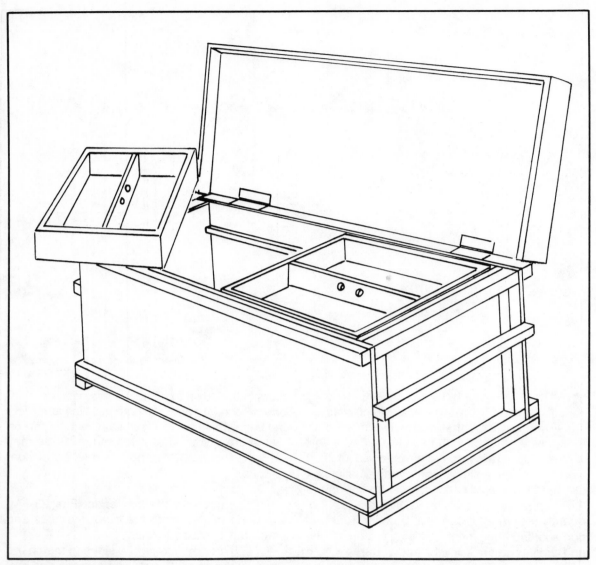

Fig. 23-1. A plywood tool box with lift-out trays.

made with strips of wood across (Fig. 23-3E). Round the parts that will be gripped before screwing them on.

6. There are three possible ways of making the lid. Plywood without edge stiffening might buckle. There could be a ½-inch plywood top with strips under the edges (Fig. 23-2C), or the plywood can be stiffened inside and strips put outside (Fig. 23-2D), or ¾-inch plywood might be used without stiffening (Fig. 23-2E and 3F). The last two methods hide the ply edges, which may be vulnerable to damp. Make the lid slightly bigger than the outside of the box and put strips on three edges only. Hinges go along the other side (Fig. 23-3G).

7. Take the sharpness off all external corners of the box and its lid.

8. The old craftsman's box had many

110

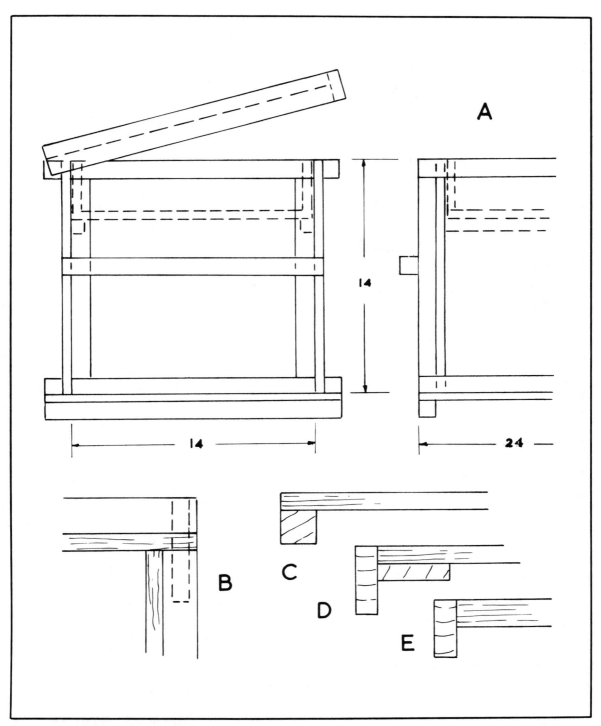

Fig. 23-2. Sizes and sections for the tool box.

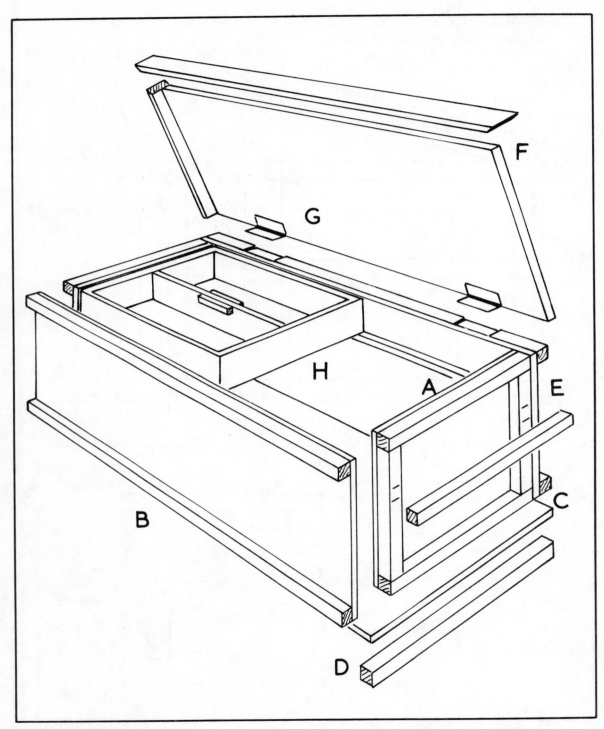

Fig. 23-3. Tool box parts.

trays and compartments. A plain box may suit your needs, but one or more trays at the top will hold small items that could be lost among big tools below. Two trays are suggested. They fill the top, but if one is lifted out, the other can be slid along (Fig. 23-3H). Put strips on the box sides to support them.

9. Any joints may be used at the corners of the trays. If they are without divisions to grip, put finger holes in the ends for lifting out. If you include one or more divisions, there can be thickening at the center of the top edge to provide a grip.

Materials List for Toolbox

2 ends	14	× 14	× ½	plywood
2 sides	14	× 24	× ½	plywood
1 bottom	17	× 24	× ½	plywood
8 end frames	1	× 1	× 15	
4 side frames	1	× 1	× 25	
2 handles	1	× 1	× 16	
2 feet	1	× 1	× 18	
1 lid	18	× 25	× ¾	plywood
2 lid edges	⅝	× 2	× 19	
10 tray parts	½	× 3	× 15	
2 tray bottoms	12	× 14	× ¼	plywood
2 tray bearers	⅝	× ⅝	× 24	

24

Sawing Aids

WHEN USING A HAND SAW, A PORTABLE CIRCU-
lar saw or a chain saw, it is important that
the wood being worked cannot move. While this
is important for accuracy, it is essential for safety
if you are using a power saw. Yet, wood is often
insecurely supported. A saw buck is best when
cutting logs, and something better than a tem-
porarily nailed-together improvisation is advisable. For work on boards or sheet material it is
best to have firm supports at a convenient level,
and saw horses or trestles have many other uses
as well in a shop or on a building site. Two examples you can make are shown (Fig. 24-1).

Both supports could be made of softwood,
which would be light, but for frequent and heavy
use it would be better to use a close-grained
hardwood. Joints should be made with glue and
stout screws or bolts through in a few places.

SAW BUCK

The *saw buck* (Fig. 24-2A) has legs made from
2-inch-by-4-inch section and the other parts are
1-inch-by-3-inch. The sizes are designed to accommodate logs about 6 inches diameter, but
larger and smaller ones will fit.

The legs make an angle of 50° with the
ground, which gives a good hold on a log without the excessive spread of feet often seen when
the legs cross squarely. Shallow notches lock
the leg crossings.

1. Make two pair of legs (Fig. 24-2B). Tops
are square, but cut feet at 50° and take off the
sharp point. Cut the notches ½-inch deep and
use the actual wood to set the width to mark.
Mark on the edges where the other pieces come.

2. Join the legs with glue and a ½-inch
bolt through the center of the crossing. Check
that the ends match.

3. Join the ends with the straight pieces
(Fig. 24-2C), using glue and at least two screws
at each crossing. Put temporary pieces across
the feet to keep the ends square and parallel.

4. Make the outer diagonals (Fig. 24-2D)
for each side and add them while the assembly

Fig. 24-1. A saw buck and a sawing horse or trestle.

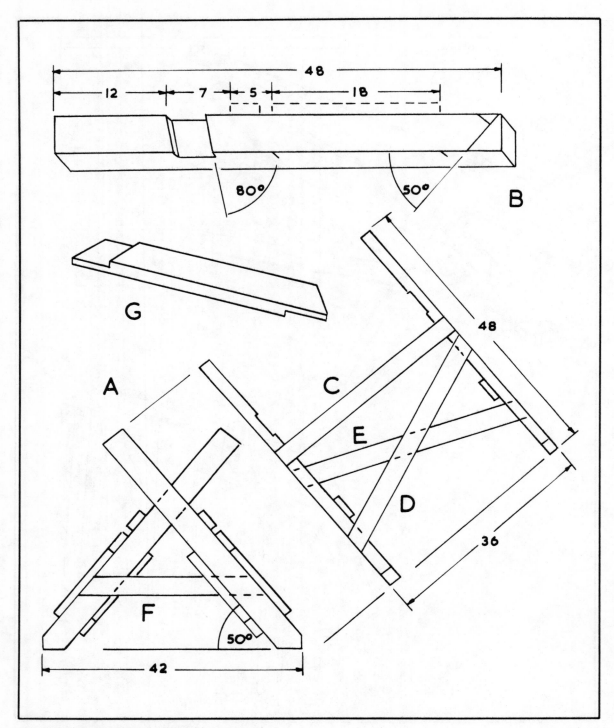

Fig. 24-2. Constructional details of the saw buck.

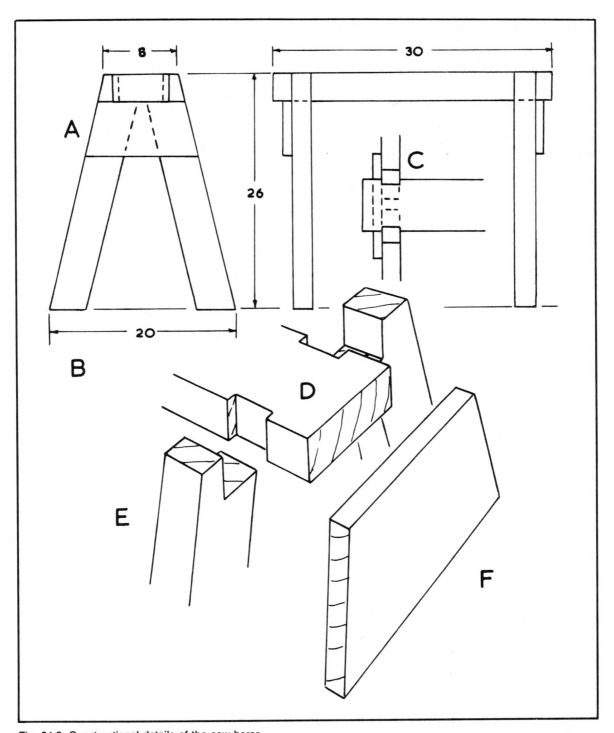

Fig. 24-3. Constructional details of the saw horse.

is standing on a flat surface. The wood may be cut too long to trim later.

5. Do the same with the inner diagonals (Fig. 24-2E).

6. The cross braces (Fig. 24-2F) should be arranged about midway between the joints of the diagonal braces. Mark the wood in position. Cut ½ inch from each side (Fig. 24-2G), so the brace goes squarely across when screwed in position.

Materials List for Saw Buck

4 legs	2 × 4 × 50
2 cross pieces	1 × 3 × 38
4 diagonals	1 × 3 × 44
2 braces	1 × 3 × 36

SAW HORSE

The *saw horse* or *trestle* (Fig. 24-3A) is a type of sawing support with a top wide enough to be used for many purposes singly, but when dealing with large pieces, such as sheets of plywood, it is better to have a pair. The legs are shown close to the ends, to reduce the risk to tipping when working over the edge.

1. Cut the wood to size and check the actual measurements, then set out the main lines of an end view (Fig. 24-3B) to get the angles to cut the legs.

2. Make the top with notches ½-inch deep for the legs (Fig. 24-3C and D).

3. Cut the tops of the legs to fit into the notches and extend 1 inch outside them (Fig. 24-3E), using the angle obtained from your setting out.

4. Mark the bottoms of the legs, but delay cutting them until after assembly, when they can be checked and cut together in case there are any slight variations that would affect standing level.

5. Glue and screw the legs to the top and add the bracing pieces outside (Fig. 24-3F).

Materials List for Saw Horse

1 top	3 × 6 × 32
4 legs	2 × 4 × 30
2 braces	1 × 6 × 14

Index

The Book Club offers a wood identification kit that includes 30 samples of cabinet woods. For details on ordering, please write: Book Club, Member Services, P.O. Box 2033, Latham, N.Y. 12111.